RV LIVING PASSIVE INCOME

Quit Your Daily Job, RV Living and Start Your Laptop Lifestyle using Passive Income Strategies + 7 Secret Rules For Investing After Retirement

TABLE OF CONTENTS

INTRODUCTION

Chapter 1: HOW TO MAKE MONEY FULL-TIME RVING

Chapter 2: TIPS TO SAVE A LOT OF MONEY AND LIVE COMFORTABLY LIVING IN A CAMPER RV

Chapter 3: SETTING UP A COST COMPARISON

Chapter 4: KEY RETIREMENT-PLANNING STEPS EVERYONE SHOULD TAKE

Chapter 5: BEST RV LOANS

Chapter 6: BEST STATES FOR FULL-TIME RV LIVING (2021)

Chapter 7: TIPS TO SAVE A LOT OF MONEY AND LIVE COMFORTABLY

Chapter 8: 20 WAYS TO MAKE MONEY WHILE FULL-TIME RVING

Chapter 9: MYTHS ABOUT PASSIVE INCOME YOU CAN'T AFFORD TO BELIEVE

Chapter 10: RVING WITH A PET

Chapter 11: RVING WITH KIDS

Chapter 12: RV MISTAKES YOU NEED TO AVOID

Chapter 13: SECRET RULES FOR INVESTING AFTER RETIREMENT

CONCLUSION

INTRODUCTION

Consider a life in which you are not required to report to work at 9 a.m. You can work from the comfort of your own home and choose your schedule. Are you visualizing it? Wonderful.

However, there is more...

You have freedom, freedom to travel wherever your heart desires.

Perhaps you've had a dream destination in your mind for years, only to put it off until next summer, when you hope to have the time and money.

However, what if I told you that there was a way to visit that ideal place this year and that you could even bring your job with you? This is not a scene from Hollywood, but possible for you.

What is Passive Income?

Passive income is money earned that does not require a great deal of "active" labor to maintain. In essence, you can do the most of the work up front and then supplement your income with some more effort along the way.

For instance, if you build an online course, all you need to do is maintain the information updated to keep the revenue flowing.

You've probably heard the phrase "earn money while you sleep." That is the main incentive for people to pursue passive income.

You can create something (a course, ebook, blog, videos, or an online store) that generates revenue even while you are not actively working. Alternatively, you can invest in passive income investments (real estate or stocks) that allow you to earn money passively.

Which Is Best for Me: Active Income or Passive Income?

In theory, all of your sources of revenue are equivalent in importance. However, when it comes to financial independence, passive income far outpaces active income.

As you can see, active income is the money earned by the current efforts you are making. And you must continue working in order to generate an income. If you resign, you will not be compensated. Your time is directly proportional to your earnings.

Then there is passive income. A source of income that does not demand your personal participation. And the funds continue to pour in for years. If you want to create a financially independent dream life, it may be best to focus on passive income.

Bear in mind that, while you can create a passive income stream with a minimal investment, you are making no less of a commitment than someone investing their time. Creating passive income that is similar to revenue gained through active efforts requires a good amount of work upfront.

By working online and becoming your employer, you can avoid being confined to a single place. You can quit and immerse yourself in the adventurous world of RV living.

We often see influencers on YouTube or Instagram who travel full-time and inspire us to think, "Wow. If only that were me. They are having a good time!" Yes, they are. But so can you!

Explore the best ways to earn passive income, why everyone can earn passive income, and debunk common myths surrounding passive income.

CHAPTER 1: HOW TO MAKE MONEY FULL-TIME RVING

Many people have inquired about earning money while traveling in an RV. And, since van life has grown in popularity, I decided to look into the best ways to make a living in a van.

So, in this chapter, I'll reveal my 23 money-making ideas for RV travelers.

Why would you live in a RV?

Not everyone is cut out for a desk job. Many of us fantasize about roaming from one location to another and traveling around the world.

It is a popular belief that only wealthy people can travel all year without thinking about money.

This is a myth.

To be honest, you don't have to be a millionaire to keep traveling across the world.

Living in a RV can be a very cost-effective way to save money and live on a shoestring budget.

How do RVers make money while traveling?

The current global economic climate has made it much easier for us to travel in an RV and live in a van while still earning money.

For some, generating money while traveling in an RV is a pastime, while for others, earning money while traveling in a van or an RV has become a full-time job.

For individuals looking to generate money while traveling in an RV, there are numerous job options accessible.

The following 23 job suggestions will show you how to make money while living in a van or RV.

Here's how to make money while traveling in an RV without wasting any time.

1. Work at Campground or Festival

Working at a campground is one way to make money while traveling in an RV.

Camping has been a seasonal job for certain people for a long time.

It is one of the most effective ways to earn money while traveling.

You can work at campgrounds whenever you stop by one. They are always in need of assistance with one thing or the other.

Working as a campground host is also an option. This job is for persons who enjoy camping and have always wanted to be in charge of one.

This will make up for your low rent, plus you'll have a place to do your laundry as well.

2. Work as Bartender While Traveling

The job of a bartender is never dull. As a result, many people consider working as a bartender while traveling to be a viable option.

Working as a bartender while traveling has the benefit of allowing you to attend some of the coolest parties in your destination.

Furthermore, bartenders do not require any additional training or experience. You can work for only a few hours and still make a great living.

3. Get a Workamping Job

Workamping is perhaps one of the most important aspects of RV travel. It's a part of your RV lifestyle.

For those unaware, workamping is the act of exchanging services in exchange for a free campground or a salary.

Many people falsely believe that work camping is only for retirees.

However, they do not realize that this is also one of the simplest ways to make money.

Work camping is everything you've hoped for and more. It is one of the most important means of earning money while traveling.

You don't need a resume.

4. Domestic Cleaning While Living in a Van

There is always a need for domestic assistance. Finding domestic cleaning is straightforward when you are traveling.

Many people are looking for someone to help them with the dishes, laundry, gardening, or other household duties.

If you ever find yourself in a scenario where you need to make quick money while traveling, household cleaning is a good option.

You do not have to ask for money in exchange for the domestic assistance you provide.

You can even request a place to stay, a location to do your laundry for a few weeks or months, or a delicious home-cooked meal.

You can plan to work at a certain house as well as at several others down the neighborhood.

Domestic cleaning does not have to be limited to cleaning; you can also work as a babysitter and earn some money.

5. Be a Travel Photographer

It's no secret that travel photographers make a good living.

If you have a professional camera or even just the ability to take great images, travel photography should be one of your options for making money.

All you have to do is take creative photographs of some of the country's most prominent tourist sites and interesting local spots. Then, you can share it on Instagram and stock photo sites.

These photos can even be sold to a magazine, website, or newspaper. You must also establish your style to distinguish yourself.

This way, you can build your portfolio too. In some situations, you may even be able to show your portfolio to potential clients.

You can then take photos of other people, which is another way to make money while traveling in an RV.

6. Find Jobs on Craigslist

If you are having trouble making ends meet while traveling, you should look for a craigslist job.

Craigslist is a job-advertising website that lists a variety of job openings. It features sections dedicated to a variety of things you need.

All you have to do is submit your resume, and you'll be able to contact people who are looking for work.

Getting a job on Craigslist while traveling might be convenient.

You do not need to put your sightseeing or travel plans on hold to attend job interviews or hunt for work.

You can even find jobs online and work on them from the comfort of your RV. Craigslist enables you to make a lot of money with very little effort.

7. Thrift Store and Garage Sale Items on eBay

Keep an eye out for deals at thrift stores and garage sales while you're on the road. You can flip these finds on eBay for a good profit.

Since you are traveling in an RV and living in a van, some items are no longer useful.

You can make money while traveling by selling that item or product on eBay.

Before you decide to offer a product, you should make sure it is of good quality.

8. Rent Out Your RV

People are becoming more interested in RV living year after year. Many people love to travel around in a recreational vehicle (RV).

If you already have one and are traveling on it, you can use it to make money. Renting out your RV has several benefits.

To begin with, you will be able to earn some extra cash.

If you are traveling alone and have the RV to yourself, you can rent out your RV to a group or family.

You can even offer to be the driver.

You can even rent it out online if you have difficulty finding people.

9. Work at National Park

The national park employs seasonal workers every year.

People are needed in national parks to educate visitors, conduct research, protect the park's well-being, and welcome visitors.

The national park is large and in need of assistance. Some of these jobs are close to RV sites.

If you are traveling via RV, you can take advantage of this opportunity to volunteer.

You can check the national parks website to see any seasonal opportunities available and apply right away.

10. Manage Real Estate Properties

If you want to make money while living in a van, consider managing real estate properties.

Many homeowners are too preoccupied with their rental properties to deal with them. They require a personal assistant to help them maintain their Airbnb properties and find renters.

This is where you can offer your services. It'll be your responsibility to coordinate with those looking for an Airbnb or a place to stay.

You can show them around. You should coordinate with the house cleaners and ensure that everything is in order.

11. Dog Sitting/ Dog Walking

Dog sitting and dog walking are fantastic ways to make money when you live in a van or travel in an RV.

You will also have the opportunity to stay at home for a few days because you will be looking after other people's pets.

You can use Rover or just create a website to advertise your dog-sitting services.

The space and area don't matter while you are dog sitting. You can choose your rates based on whatever best suits you.

12. Food Deliveries

The best part about having an RV can move around quickly. You do not need to be concerned about transportation.

You can transport food from restaurants using your RV.

UberEATS and Postmates, for example, are always looking for someone to assist them in delivering food to their clients.

It's as simple as picking up the food order from the restaurant and delivering it to the customer's door.

13. Deliver Amazon Parcels in your RV

You can now deliver Amazon packages in your RVs, thanks to Amazon.

This is one way to make money while living in a van. Amazon offers a Camper Force program where RVers pick, pack, stow, and transport products for the company.

If you decide to do this, you will earn money on an hourly basis.

You can earn completion and referral bonuses by enrolling in the program. Amazon's Camper Force initiative is only available for a limited time.

So, if you're seeking a seasonal job, this could be a fantastic option.

You can even spend a few days living at one of Amazon's warehouses.

14. Start a Travel Blog

One of the most creative ways to make money while living in a van is to start a travel blog.

If you are always on the go, you should start a travel blog because it will thrive.

You can make posts about places you are visiting. You can be very inventive and create highly artistic-looking websites that users will enjoy reading and viewing.

You can make money from your blog by advertising, sponsorships, affiliate marketing, reviews, etc.

Travel blogs aren't easy to get rich right away, but they are fun to keep things interesting.

15. Social Media Influencer

Becoming an influencer has been thriving all over the world.

The nicest part about becoming a social media influencer is that you can earn six figures and have your travel expenses covered.

When you opt to travel as a social media influencer, you will discover that most of your travels are sponsored and paid for.

This means you won't have to worry about money while you're on vacation.

All you need is a social media account, perhaps on Instagram or Facebook, with a large number of followers, and you're good to go.

16. YouTube Channel on Travel

Over the years, travel vlogs have become increasingly popular among the general public.

If you're looking for a way to augment your income, starting a YouTube channel dedicated to travel is one way to do so.

When you reach a certain amount of subscribers, YouTube begins to pay you.

If you want to establish your own travel YouTube channel, make sure you keep things interesting.

You can do this by posting vlogs every day.

You can be more creative with your content by depicting the actual travel experience rather than what people imagine it to be.

17. Write an eBook about Living in a Van

Living in a van can be an awesome feeling to live in a van. It's an experience which not everyone has, and that's what makes it unique.

If you want to make money while living in a van, you can write about your experiences.

You could create short stories on eBooks or perhaps a novel about what it's like to live in a van.

All you have to do is devote some time to being creative and improving your writing skills.

If you decide to write about the experience, it could be a unique experience for many people.

18. Start Podcast About Van Life

Starting a podcast won't be as difficult if you already have a travel blog.

However, if you don't have a blog, you shouldn't be too worried.

However, if you don't have a blog, you shouldn't be too worried. People earn money through podcasts too.

There are websites where you can register and start recording your podcast. You can talk about your travels and what it's like to live in an RV.

You can even turn your podcast into a guide for individuals interested in adopting the RV lifestyle.

Starting a podcast has the advantage of providing you with an audience regardless of what they are doing. A podcast can be listened to at any time by anyone. You can make money through via a podcast by advertisements and getting sponsorships.

You can also make money by promoting other people's products.

19. Become an Affiliate Marketer

Traveling and becoming an affiliate marketer are inextricably linked.

An affiliate marketer promotes a company or business by using or showcasing its products.

When you work as an affiliate marketer, you won't find a sponsor for your trip, but you will earn money while on it.

This is because you are also advertising for the sponsor.

You won't have to worry about your travel expenses as you can augment your income as an affiliate marketer.

You can market for the destination you intend to travel to.

If you plan on marketing a company like Adidas, they also provide you with material assistance.

Entrepreneur John Crestani built a $500K-per-month business while traveling the world thanks to affiliate marketing.

20. Work as a Day Laborer

Working in a van may be a fun and rewarding experience.

If you need money, but your travel schedule is tight, you can work as a day laborer while traveling in an RV.

Day laborers are people who are employed on a temporary, day-to-day basis. A temporary labor agency can help you find work.

You can work on a construction site or assist with deliveries.

21. Become a Virtual Assistant

Being a virtual assistant has become more popular than ever before, thanks to the internet and smart devices.

Many people prefer to telecommute. Executives can now rely on assistants who may be working remotely from somewhere else thanks to the internet.

If you want to earn money while traveling in your RV, this is a great opportunity.

You can work independently on websites like Upwork and Freelancer.

You can create and write content for various websites and companies.

Apart from that, you can work on your travel business.

This should be an easy task for you if you already have travel experience.

This includes making hotel reservations, flight reservations, and even planning the entire day for the traveler.

22. Teach Online While Traveling

Making money while traveling has become easier thanks to the internet's tenacity.

You can also teach students online. You can choose to show a specific language, such as English, and teach students how to read, write, and even speak it.

You can sign up for visits such as DaDa, iTutorGroup, and even GoKidGo, which offer you the opportunity to teach English online.

If you have gone to another country, you can teach people a language from your country, such as French, Hindi, or Dutch.

Some websites need teachers for home tutoring or other purposes.

You can sign up for those websites and help students with assignments, homework, exams, and other schoolwork.

23. Online Surveys to Earn Money

Earning money via reliable survey sites is easy. It's arguably the simplest way to earn money while traveling.

Some websites pay you to do surveys in exchange for money.

You won't have to spend a lot of time filling out online surveys, so you won't have to worry about wasting time trying to make money.

You can fill out online surveys while on the move.

It also does not require a lot of effort. You only need to register on one of the websites, and you are good to go.

Some companies will send you an email with information about their surveys.

The reward varies from one to the next; some offer points that may be redeemed for cash.

When living in an RV, you must be willing to try new things.

Taking a trip in an RV is an experience itself. However, you never know what chances it may present.

The best thing about traveling in an RV is that you never have to worry about finding a place to stay as you will always have a place to stay.

It's simple to make money while traveling in your RV.

There are numerous work opportunities available to you. You can also use your travel experience to learn more about yourself.

With many different job options available to you while traveling, you can pursue your other interests also.

Earning money while traveling will help you fund your trip and enhance your overall travel experience.

CHAPTER 2: TIPS TO SAVE A LOT OF MONEY AND LIVE COMFORTABLY LIVING IN A CAMPER RV

The cost of living in a house can be quite high.

Saving money seems to be almost impossible.

It can also make achieving your financial goals incredibly challenging.

That is why more individuals are considering moving into a camper van than ever before!

The RV lifestyle isn't entirely new. It is, however, not as expected or standard as one might believe. Which is strange because, let's face it, who wouldn't want to do it?

It's entertaining, exciting, and financially beneficial.

A lot of travel enthusiasts prefer to live in an RV to save money and be on the road worry-free, and to be honest, isn't that the kind of Instagram-worthy life we all secretly wish for?

Living in an RV can help you live a debt-free, happier, and wealthy life—a very amazing experience.

However, because of the magical nature of this lifestyle, there are a few practical considerations to make.

If you're thinking about living in an RV full-time to save money, there are a few things you should be aware of.

In this chapter, you'll find all of these things and much more.

Does living in an RV save money?

It does! You're saving on rent, you're not getting huge electricity and gas bills, and you're not paying any house taxes, all of which add up to a big chunk of your monthly living costs.

Many people believe that living in a house trailer helps them prevent and pay off debts and loans. Because your whole lifestyle becomes much more compact, you just use what you need and only pay for what you use.

Overall, living in an RV can save you hundreds of thousands of dollars per month.

You can put all your savings toward paying off debts, investing wherever you wish, going to college or university, and so on.

What Should You Consider Before A Living In An RV Full-Time To Save Money?

So, you are saving money, making your life easier, and spending the happiest days of your life by camping, traveling, and having all the adventures you want!

Why Choose to Live in an RV?

People prefer to live in RVs for a variety of reasons all around the world. And for some of them, it's all about saving money!

Living in an RV is a good way to see the country! But will it save you money?

For many people who can't afford traditional homeownership, living in an RV to save money is a feasible and viable option. Some people also live in RVs to place a greater emphasis on experiences rather than material possessions. Others do it to travel around the country.

Of course, some people prefer to live in an RV for the reasons stated above. Yes, you can do it, too!

Full-Time Stationary RV Living

Full-time stationary RV life entails living in an RV full-time in one spot or a general location, such as a long-term RV park. Those who choose to live in fixed RVs must remain in the same location for work, school, or other obligations.

In this situation, long-term RV parks are an excellent low-cost option for saving money while living in an RV. If these parks are not available, you can always go from park to park within the same area. This may not be the most cost-effective alternative.

Full-Time RV Living and Traveling

You could live in your RV while traveling full-time rather than taking up a semi-permanent station at an RV park. This, believe it or not, can save you just as much (if not more) money as staying in a long-term RV park.

How is that possible given the high cost of travel? Any full-time RVer will tell you that it doesn't have to be!

For many full-time RVers, the only significant living expenses are gas and the occasional campsite fees. Many areas in the United States allow free camping, making this a very inexpensive way to travel around the country.

How Much Does It Cost to Live in an RV?

Living in an RV can be as expensive or as inexpensive as you want it to be—no two people (or families) RV alike. RVers, like people who live in regular houses, have different lifestyle preferences.

Many RVers prefer to stay in luxury RV resorts with amenities, such as heated pools, private patios, and private casitas. Others prefer boondocking in the desert with no hookups, no amenities, and no neighbors for miles.

Full-time RVers are often boondocking in the desert during the winter.

If you travel slowly, you will spend less money on gas. It's just another cost of living, like rent or utilities.

Although there is no actual answer to how much it costs to live in an RV, here are some examples from full-time RVers:

As you can see, living a decent RV lifestyle for roughly $2,000-$3,000 per month is achievable, especially if you invest in upgrades to make boondocking easier!

How to Save Money by Living in an RV

While living in an RV, there are numerous ways to save money. We've listed our top tips here.

Join Discount Camping Memberships

First and foremost, sign up for discounted camping memberships! There are a plethora of options available, all of which will save you money.

Boondockers Welcome is a camping membership program that allows you to camp for free with participating hosts across the country who welcome RVers passing through.

Harvest Hosts offers free overnight stays at places like vineyards, wineries, museums, and more.

Thousand Trails is a discount camping club that can help you save a lot of money at campgrounds all through the United States.

Passport America is only $44 per year and saves you 50 percent at participating campgrounds. This camping membership pays for itself within the first two usages.

Low-Price RV Parks

When booking RV parks and campgrounds, look around for the best deal! State park campgrounds are the best place to find low nightly rates.

For highly discounted rates, book weekly or monthly stays rather than nightly stays.

Boondocking

Boondocking is probably the best method to save money while RVing. Dry camping is another name for this style of camping. That's camping without access to electricity, running water, or sewer hookups.

You can lawfully camp for free on most Bureau of Land Management (BLM) and National Forest land around the United States. Many full-time RVers take advantage of this land to save money when traveling.

Many full-time RVers take advantage of this land to save money when traveling.

Tips for Boondocking

Dry camping is a fantastic experience. You get to stay in stunning locations and enjoy seclusion that you may have only imagined. However, there are a few upgrades you can make to your RV to make it more comfortable.

Installing solar panels on your RV and replacing your RV batteries will provide you with more electricity for longer periods, so you won't feel like you are roughing it.

Additionally, consider switching to a composting toilet to become more self-sufficient and eliminate the need to dump black water. After you convert, you can even convert your black water tank to extra grey water storage.

Travel Slowly

Traveling slowly can help you save money on gas. When you spend more time in one place, you have more time to explore it like a local. This is one of the most appealing parts of RVing!

Prepare Your Food

Eating out all the time gets expensive. It's costly! If you are still looking for an RV, the kitchen is an important part. Choose a kitchen layout that encourages you to prepare meals at home, thereby saving you money in the long term.

Cooking in your RV is a cost-effective way to save money.

Practice Minimalism

Minimalism is non-negotiable when you live in an RV. You can't buy much since you don't have anywhere to store it! Simple living, which entails deferring purchases until you're certain you can't live without them, is a certain way to save money while RVing.

Will Living in an RV Save You Money?

If you live thoughtfully, you can save money while living in an RV, even while traveling. However, if you choose to stay in luxury RV parks and spend money on meals and experiences, it may be just as expensive (if not more so) as a stationary life. There is no right or wrong in this situation. It is entirely up to you and your lifestyle preferences to save money.

Now, let's look at everything you should consider before buying an RV.

The following list highlights some of the most important and frequently overlooked considerations to make before committing to this lifestyle.

Here are my 14 money-saving and debt-free tips for living in a camper RV:

1. Do your research before purchasing your RV

Purchasing an RV to live in is a great but costly investment. So, before you get one, make sure you know what you want and what you're getting yourself into.

Before you go out looking for a vehicle and eventually buying one, do your research and take the time to learn about them.

When it comes to preparing to live in an RV, there are many things to consider. A few examples being:

- The price of the RV
- The size of the RV
- The features and benefits you're looking for
- How much stuff you own and have to take along
- The quality levels of the vehicle
- What company you want to go for
- What designs, style, and colors of trailer you want
- Know how you are going to use the trailer
- Do you want brand new or pre-used RVs?

2. Do not drive an RV with full tanks

While various people have different views and opinions on the safety of traveling with full or empty water tanks, one thing is certain: full tanks are always heavier. An RV often transports 20-100 gallons of water, which is a considerable amount of weight in pounds and kilograms!

There's only so much weight your vehicle can pull and still drive smoothly, based on its towing capability and weight tolerance.

The more weight you put on your trailer, the more fuel it consumes to keep it running. The faster it burns through the fuel, the sooner you'll have to refill it. Overall, this process can be quite costly, especially if you live in an RV to save money.

3. Do not run your RV appliances on propane

For several reasons, using propane and running your RV appliances on is an unpopular recommendation.

To begin with, it can be dangerous. You live in a mobile home, which means that everything, including your appliances, is constantly moving. If one of the machines fails for some reason, the propane will leak. Because propane is highly flammable, even the tiniest spark can ignite it; this leak is extremely dangerous.

Furthermore, propane can be quite costly, especially when the appliances are used full-time or when you're moving. You can save money by avoiding the usage of this fuel.

4. Try to stay in one place

You're probably only willing to start to live in an RV because you want to keep moving. However, as exciting and entertaining as that may sound, it is not entirely practical.

You see, even if you have the opportunity to move at any time, it is always advisable to stay put whenever possible. The reason for this is that when you stay stable and fixed, the risks of being on the road are reduced to a minimum (this may seem obvious, but hear me out!) On the road, there is a lower risk of propane leakage, accidents, running out of fuel or food, and a variety of other unpleasant events. It also cuts down the costs of constantly traveling, such as gasoline tank refills, dining out, and so on. As a result, staying put for longer periods is significantly less expensive than constantly moving.

5. Travel lightly when RV living

As we stated right now, living in an RV to save money is all about making life more comfortable and straightforward. So, make sure you travel light. Take only what you require and discard the rest. YoOu do not need that oversized couch or the 28-inch TV; get rid of it! Take food, clothes, and the necessities of life, but don't hoard. You're already on the journey! You can acquire anything you need just on the street; there's a grocery shop or gas station on every corner.

Not only is traveling light less expensive and stressful, but it also reduces the burden on the trailer, making it run more smoothly and efficiently. The less work a vehicle has to expend, the more fuel it will use efficiently. Fuel efficiency is, in turn, a cost-effective benefit. Consider everything with a more open mind and a longer-term perspective.

6. Find cheap camping sites and parking spaces

One of the best things about living in a trailer is that you can park it almost anywhere—note the word "almost"; we'll get to that in a moment.

Look for low-cost or no-cost parking lots for your RV, as well as low-cost or no-cost camping spots. Specific camping sites charge money but provide facilities services such as food and safety. You can look for free camping spots if you don't think you need either and don't want to spend the extra cash.

Pro tip: these camping spots are easy to locate on the internet. Simply go to Google and search for free camping areas in your neighborhood, or if you have a sharp eye, you can find some fantastic low-key campgrounds that are not yet open to the public.

I chose the word "almost" because some parking places, such as grocery stores, motels, petrol stations, and casinos, only allow RVs and trailers to stay for a few hours.

In such cases, you must get authorization from authorities, management, or the owner, as well as parking allowance guidelines.

Cashback credit cards are another wonderful method to save money and live a more affordable mobile lifestyle.

Renting RVs and paying for fuel using this method offers its own set of advantages, which includes the following:

- They assist you in better managing your finances.

- They give rewards for spending money. These rewards can be redeemed and used on food or other amenities.

- Perks and offers come in handy from time to time, especially when you're trying to save money.

- They are far more convenient to use and maintain than conventional credit cards. Many people prefer to use this payment option as beginners instead of starting with a credit or debit card.

7. Eat in or outside your RV

The primary and most common motivation for many people's choice to remain in an RV is to save money. Consider how much money you can save on meals in addition to the rent and bills you're saving.

It is fine to indulge now and then, but try to avoid eating out or ordering unnecessary restaurant food regularly. Instead, focus on cooking for yourself and dining inside or outside the trailer.

A lot of RVs have special spaces for tables and chairs. If not, you can always get some of those foldable, travel-friendly items and make a nice outdoor seating arrangement for yourself and your traveling partner.

This will help you save money in the long term!

9. Use a camping membership to save money

Some campgrounds and RV parks provide memberships for RV owners if you don't know what they are.

They provide services and facilities (which vary depending on the campground) in exchange for a one-time fee or annual costs (campground fees can be different also).

If you don't like the concept of traveling all the time seeking safe spots to park and stay, a long-term membership with a site like this is a brilliant idea.

Camping memberships provide you with the convenience of having a safe spot to stay for the most part while simply requiring a one-time payment.

Different campgrounds provide different services, facilities, and convenient features, and you can choose the "deal" that best meets your needs.

10. Avoid toll roads

Paying tolls charges is probably not a major concern for you if you aren't a frequent traveler. If you are always on the road, or live on it, like in this instance, stopping and paying at toll roads is inconvenient.

Choose free roads instead of going through this process every hour or so. You should do this not just for the sake of convenience but also because many regular drivers and travelers choose to use toll roads for a variety of reasons. It's not as inconvenient for them. They don't find it as inconvenient. As a result, the free roads are typically less congested and free to use.

11. Get good at RV DIY

Living in an RV has several advantages, one of which is that you improve your self-help skills. And, to be honest, it is an absolute necessity rather than a bonus. RVs can be difficult and expensive to maintain, and if you don't know much about them, consider how much money you'll be spending on routine maintenance, repairs, and general checkups.

Therefore, knowing your car is significant. More significantly, you should be aware of a few quick and easy DIYs that you can use to solve your trailer's common problems without having to call a professional every time.

Furthermore, there is no guarantee that you will come across an expert on the road. So, in case of an emergency, you're on your own. Learn the fundamentals of RV mechanics and improve your DIY skills to ensure that such a circumstance does not intimate or overwhelm you.

12. Find Free Activities

Another fantastic approach to save money while traveling is to avoid spending a lot of money on expensive and extravagant activities. Instead, look for more convenient and cost-effective options.

Instead of dining at a five-star restaurant, you might opt to eat at a more local and low-key restaurant.

These restaurants are not only more budget-friendly and inexpensive, but they also serve the most unique and delicious local cuisine!

13. Don't fuel up on the highway

Highway fuel stations may be quite costly. These expenses can mount up to a lot in the long run, and I mean a lot. So, the best thing to do is think outside the box and save all that money. Avoid doing your shopping or filling up your gas tank on the highway. Rather, fill up your gas tank before heading to the highway.

14. Perform regular checks on your RV

If you're going to embark on a long journey and aren't sure whether you'll have access to professional assistance or a garage, it's a good idea to conduct a comprehensive check on your vehicle.

Check the fuel, the fuel lines, the wheels, the appliances, the RV's exterior, and everything else you can think of that could cause you problems.

Even if you don't think a particular part of your vehicle is faulty, check it anyway.

Better safe than sorry, right?

The financial benefit of doing this frequently is that thorough periodic checkups can quickly identify problems. If a minor problem becomes a major one, you'll end up spending a lot more money than you intended to save. As a result, doing frequent checks might save you a lot of money in the long term.

Frequently Asked Questions

Why should you consider saving money while living in an RV?

There are reasons why you should consider living in a travel trailer to save money, and these reasons are what attract people to the RV lifestyle. The following are a few of the most important:

It is less expensive.

As previously said, switching to an RV lifestyle can save you a lot of money on a monthly and annual basis. Naturally, if you are trying to save money, pay off debt, or don't want to spend so much money on things you don't need, switching to an RV is a very cost-effective and economical solution.

It's simpler.

Life is a lot simpler and easier When you only have what you need and only want what you need - if that makes any sense! People with this mindset are often comfortable living in a mobile trailer to save money and simplify their lives. They just buy what they need and what they have space for. Thus, overspending is a myth for RV owners!

You are free!

If you're a fun-loving, adventurous travel enthusiast who prefers to be on the road, what better lifestyle choice than living in a moving house? Nothing surpasses the convenience of being able to go anywhere you want, with whatever you want, without having to worry about your home being left unattended. You can stay in exciting and cool places for as long as you like, and you can move about whenever you want. Furthermore, you don't have to worry about flights or transportation costs, so living in an RV is far less expensive than flying or taking other modes of transportation.

It's more convenient.
Again, if you frequently travel, living in an RV can save you a lot of stress, effort, and money. How? Consider how much money you'll save on flights, transportation, and hotel rent. Don't forget about the food costs as well.

When you live in a moving trailer, you have your bed, only have to pay for gas, and you already have all of the food you'll need. It's that simple!

Last but not least, if you enjoy camping, you'll be happy to know that living in a trailer allows you to have campfires any day of the week! Isn't it exciting? For those who enjoy an adventurous, impulsive, and exotic lifestyle, this mobile lifestyle is the best thing that has ever happened to them.

Is it less expensive to live in an RV than in a house?

Living in a trailer rather than a full house saves money since you don't have to pay for more space or rooms, and you don't have to pay for extra bills. Similarly, you can avoid paying a lot of house taxes and other payments.

Is it less expensive to live in an RV than it is to live in an apartment?

The answer to this question is dependent on your apartment costs; if you live in a large apartment with many rooms and many bills, living in an RV will be cheaper. Even if your apartment costs an average amount, the RV lifestyle is still significantly less expensive than living in an apartment.

Keep in mind that when you get the benefits of lower rates and charges, you're also giving up a lot of extra space and comfort that you'd get in a house or apartment, so keep that in mind!

How much would it cost living in an RV year-round?

Living in a trailer might cost between $1400 to $2000 or $3000 per month on average. According to our calculations, a year in an RV will cost you between $17,000 and $40,000 on average.

Indeed, there is a significant disparity in these expenses. Still, they are dependent on various things, including your lifestyle, how much you move and travel, and what your average food costs are.

How much would it cost to live full-time in an RV park?

This amount is determined by whether you keep moving or if you have a specific campground membership.

The level of luxury in your lifestyle, such as how often you dine out, how much you shop, and what your appliances run on, greatly impacts your overall costs when living in a trailer full-time.

Parking spaces that merely allow parking but provide no services or facilities can cost between $200 to $800, sometimes even more.

These places will cost significantly more if they provide sewer maintenance, electricity, water, laundry, cable, and the internet.

Living in an RV full-time is a fantastic option to save money. However, the practical aspects of it are completely different from what you might expect.

CHAPTER 3: SETTING UP A COST COMPARISON

Which is more expensive? Living in an RV full-time vs. living at home

I'm always surprised at how many people say, "I would love to full-time in an RV, but it is just too expensive." When we
initially considered selling our home and living full-time in an RV (I am.

I recently reran them using my full-timing experiences, and the results may surprise you.

Many of life's costs are the same, but each lifestyle has its special costs. Your costs may vary, but the following is a combination of my costs or U.S. averages, assuming either an RV and one car or a house and two cars.

Home — There are two perspectives on this. You are either paying a mortgage or losing interest on a $200,000 home because your money is locked up in the house (homes as an investment tend to be risky). This works out to be $1,000 every month.

RV – Just like a house, an RV can cost a lot of money in the form of a mortgage or a lost investment. We purchased a new, very ordinary RV for roughly $400 each month.

Taxes and insurance — An RV does not require house insurance and does not require a second car. There are no license fees or taxes on them. You must account for the costs of RV insurance and fees. This amounted to a monthly savings of $100.

Utilities — When RVing, you won't have to pay for utilities such as water, electricity, natural gas, trash, sewer, or cable. All of this is included in the cost of your RV site. Phone and internet stay roughly the same. This amounted to a monthly savings of $175.

Campsites – We spent an average of $33 per night camping, which included a mixture of national, state, and RV parks, as well as some boondocking. This means a cost of $1,000 per month.

Maintenance – Although RV life necessitates maintenance on both the car and the RV, it pales compared to owning a house and two cars. According to experts, a typical homeowner spends 1-4 percent of their home's worth on maintenance. This is an estimate, but I believe we will save $150 per month.

Big items – If you own a home, you almost certainly have a lot of things you can't bring with you in your RV. We were able to sell our second car and our large lawnmower, and various other stuff such as furniture. This money was invested, making us USD100 every month.

Storage – We ended up with two storage units in two different states (don't ask) for stuff we wanted to keep. This cost us $225 a month.

Stuff – You don't buy "stuff" anymore because your RV has no room for it. So, while you might buy furniture, adorable pillows, paintings, and other home décor regularly, you don't spend money while RVing. While some people live to shop for clothes, you won't be able to do so with your closet's one-foot space for hanging garments and restricted space for shoes. I didn't buy "expensive" clothes very often, and I mostly wore jeans or shorts. I saved $175 every month.

Food – According to studies, the average American household wastes 25% of their food. This is the result of spoiled or uneaten food. When you live in an RV, you have limited space for food. It's unusual to discard something because you didn't notice it in the back of your small refrigerator. I believe you eat healthier since you spend more time outside hiking. Assuming an average $440 each month for 2 people, you save about 75USD a month.

Vacation – When you live in a house, you are more likely to spend a significant amount of money on a large vacation each year. This includes the costs of flights, accommodations, and meals. When you live in an RV full-time, every day is a vacation. You pay money for things like museums, but they aren't that expensive. I assumed that I saved 1USD25 per month.

Mail forwarding – Mail forwarding is not expensive. The service costs an average of $25 each month, including shipping.

Gasoline – The cost of gas for the RV and automobile might be substantial. Much of this is determined by how frequently you travel. It cost us an additional $250 every month.

We spent the same amount of money working through this example, whether at home or full-timing. And it was pretty much equal for us.

Your numbers may change, but don't let the cost of going full-time keep you from doing so. Traveling gave us a whole new perspective and was worth it!

Compare RV Prices: Bottom Line Cost And More

These days, an increasing number of people are dabbling in RV camping. And, like housing prices, the cost of owning a recreational vehicle has increased to all-time highs. However, there are still savings to be had if you empower yourself with information, do some research on existing models and floor plans, and understand the additional costs associated with RV ownership before you start shopping. The following are some of the factors that influence RV prices:

Cost Range of RV Types

RV types are split into 2 main groups:

Motorhomes

These are motorized vehicles and consist of:

1. Class A — The largest of the RV vehicles, with wide front windows and a bus-like look. They have diesel or gas engines and can sleep 4 to 8 people in most cases. Class As are typically 25' to 40' in length, and new vehicles can cost between $75,000 and $1,000,000 or over depending on the interior finishes and amenities ordered.

2. Class B - These are commonly referred to as vans. Engines can be diesel or gas. However, the vehicle is only comfortable for two persons.

Vans can be 17' to 24' long, and new rigs can cost between $75,000 and $150,000 or over.

3. Class C - These RVs, commonly identified as truck chassis with a bunk over the cab, may accommodate 4 to 6 people. A diesel or gasoline engine can also power them. Class Cs can be from 21' to 32' and new ones cost between $50,000 and $100,000.

Towables

Non-motorized campers (also referred to as "trailers") are towed behind a towing vehicle. They include:

1. Pop-Up and Hybrid Campers — These are campers with tent-like sides for sleeping areas that fold down into a hard-sided base. They can accommodate two to four people. Pop-ups range from 12 to 14 feet in length, and new campers can cost between $10,000 and $20,000.

2. Travel Trailers — These are rectangular in shape, full-sided, and have a front-mounted tow hitch. They can include slides that extend the living areas. These campers range from 14 feet to 40 feet in length and cost between $17,000 and $50,000.

3. Fifth Wheels - These trailers feature an elevated front area with a hitch inside the towing truck bed. They can also feature slides and are available in lengths ranging from 18 to 42 feet. New campers can cost between $40,000 to $135,000.

When comparing RV prices by type, motorhomes are often more expensive because they require a working engine (chassis) and living space (coach). However, the travel trailers and larger-sized 5th wheels can give you sticker shock as well because their interiors have become more luxurious over time.

What Other Factors Influence RV Prices Other Than Size?

Various factors contribute to the high cost of an RV. The following are the top three factor that determines the cost of a recreational vehicle:

1. Manufacturer Reputation — Knowing the level of workmanship put into a product can not only affect the price, but it may also result in a lasting and dependable product. Search RV forums and Facebook groups to find out what customers have to say about the good, the bad, and the ugly of each manufacturer's models.

2. Availability - If an RV model has a positive reputation, it is more likely to sell than those that do not. This might be a double negative for new buyers since the dealership may charge more for the popular model, and there are fewer of them available for purchase. This can be negated to some extent by purchasing the model during non-peak purchasing seasons.

3. Floorplan - Some floorplans are in high demand, resulting in higher prices. They may have an extra half bath, a kitchen island, or extra sleeping space, making them desirable, which may drive the asking price and reducing their availability on the dealer's lot.

Should I Consider Buying Used?

If high prices deter you from owning an RV, you might want to consider buying a secondhand one. Not only will the purchase price be lower, but the appraisal value will not be as low as it would be if you drove a new vehicle off the lot.

Many RV owners purchase slightly used rigs with cheaper sticker prices because the prior owner has worked out many of the "kinks." These second owners believe they will profit from lower purchase prices and fewer repair fixes because new RVs have a fair share of difficulties that are repaired under warranty.

However, if you need a loan to buy a used RV, the age of the vehicle is something to consider. Many lenders will not lend money on automobiles that are 10 years old or older, even if they are in excellent condition. Some lenders may grant you a small sum for those automobiles, but the percentage rate will be much greater, and the loan will be paid off much faster. It's usually a good idea to practice paying cash for these older vehicles.

RV Ownership Costs

With ownership comes responsibility, and a portion of your income may be used for things other than monthly loan payments, such as:

1. Taxes — You will be required to pay sales tax at the time of purchase, though many financial institutions will allow you to roll those taxes into your loan if you so desire. These are a direct outcome of the RV price you pay and the area in which you live.

2. Insurance - Insurance for newer RVs can be incredibly expensive. In the event of a repair or replacement, it makes sense to have adequate overall coverage on your insurance policy.

3. Operating Expenses — Your new recreational vehicle will not bring you very good gas mileage. In fact, motorhomes are likely to get 7 to 14 mpg, and towables may reduce your truck's mileage by a significant amount. So set aside some money for fuel, campground fees, oil changes, propane for your heater, and repairs because a moving "home" will require regular maintenance and repairs.

4. Accessories –You may decide that your RV needs leveling blocks, window awnings, new LED lights, or that the kitchen faucet has to be replaced. Keep these things in mind when you plan your budget and if looking at used vehicles.

5. Storage — If you only plan to use your RV during the summer or for a few weekend trips a year and don't have room to store it at home (or your HOA does not allow it on-site), you'll need to store your rig. Uncovered storage varies by state, but it can cost between $50 and $75 per month, while covered storage or storage with power can cost anywhere from $100 to $300 per month. How often you'll be using this new purchase and where it'll spend its "days off," and then go shopping knowing you've got a plan.

CHAPTER 4: KEY RETIREMENT-PLANNING STEPS EVERYONE SHOULD TAKE

What do you wish to do post-retirement?

Get back to your hometown and relax?

Take up some social cause?

Start a business? Or

Spend time with your family

Whatever your dream is, you must start planning now because you will no longer receive a salary or have a regular source of money once you retire. And you'll need a financial backup to cover your daily expenses and live out your golden years.

The only difference is that you continue to live after retirement, but you may not have a steady stream of money. And, to maintain your independence, you must begin saving and investing for the future now.

And don't think that having money in the bank would suffice. Mostly due to the inflation issue. Inflation is defined as an increase in the cost of goods and services. As a result of inflation, the value of your money decreases.

So, why do you need to plan for your retirement?

With a well-structured plan, you'll be equipped to deal with a variety of situations, including surpluses, shortfalls, and emergencies. You know how quickly or likely you are to reach your retirement goals. You also gain control over your cash flows, earnings and expenses, and the level of risk you must take to achieve all of your goals.

In other words, a retirement plan will enable you to develop a thorough understanding of your life goals (the ENDS) as well as the path (the MEANS) to achieving them.

Why is it necessary to plan your retirement finances?

It is easy to cover your expenses as long as you are earning your monthly salary. However, after you retire, you must have enough money saved up to live comfortably for the rest of your life.

1. To cover daily living expenses

Even after retirement, we must all cover the necessary living expenses. Because life goes on and the loss of a monthly income might be a nightmare.

Retirement planning aims to prevent this nightmare from becoming a reality. After retirement, few people receive pensions or gratuities, and even for those that do, the amount is usually insufficient to meet all of their needs.

You may ensure that your family's living level is not jeopardized after retirement by planning and accumulating a sizable retirement fund.

2. To cover medical expenses

The number of health problems and emergencies increases as one gets older. As you may be aware, medical bills have the potential to cause a hole in your wallet. Dental treatments, in particular, can be quite costly these days.

It is possible that your health insurance policy will not cover all of your medical bills.

To avoid a financial crisis in your later years, your retirement fund must be large enough to meet your and your family's medical expenses.

3. To fight inflation

Inflation is defined as an increase in the cost of goods and services. It deteriorates the purchasing power and value of your hard-earned cash.

You see, the cost of products and services has been steadily rising, and it will continue to grow until you reach retirement age.

This means you'll have to pay more in the future for everything. Everything is going to cost you more in the future, from groceries to travel to accommodation.

It would be impossible to attain all of your retirement goals without a strong retirement plan that strives to generate a suitable retirement corpus that accounts for inflation, rate of return, life expectancy, and other factors.

4. To deal with uncertainties

Life is a lot of fun, but it's also a lot of work. It can occasionally put us in unfavorable scenarios and circumstances that we weren't expecting.

Natural disasters, the loss of loved ones, financial challenges in the lives of family members, and other events have the potential to cause financial and emotional turmoil in your life.

Having a sizable corpus to deal with such unforeseen circumstances can always come to your rescue.

As a result, as you near retirement, it is essential that you have an adequate contingency fund in place so that the intermediate period of instability and turmoil can be better managed and your long-term goal of retirement is not jeopardized.

5. To meet your retirement goals

Retirement goals are the objectives you want to accomplish throughout your retirement years. These could include things like traveling and experiencing new places, as well as taking up hobbies you've always wanted to try.

However, if you do not plan and save for all of these retirement goals in your working years, they will not become a reality when you retire.

Hence, having a solid Retirement Plan that will help you understand where you are now and what measures you need to take to reach your objective is important.

Retirement planning is a multi-step, time-consuming process. You'll need to develop a financial cushion to fund a comfortable, secure—and enjoyable—retirement. The fun aspect is why it's important to pay attention to the serious (and maybe boring) phase of the process: planning how you will get there.

Thinking about your retirement goals and how long you have to achieve them is the first step in retirement planning. Then you must consider the various types of retirement accounts that can assist you in raising the funds necessary to fund your future. You must invest the money you save for it to grow. The last surprise is taxes: If you've received tax deductions for the money you've put into retirement accounts over the years, you'll be hit with a large tax bill once you start withdrawing those funds. There are strategies to keep the retirement tax hit to a minimum while you invest in the future and keep the process going when the time comes to retire.

We'll go through each of these subjects in detail here. But first, learn the five actions that everyone should follow to create a solid retirement plan regardless of age.

KEY TAKEAWAYS

• Determining time horizons, predicting expenses, calculating required after-tax returns, measuring risk tolerance, and conducting estate planning are important aspects of retirement planning.

• Start planning for retirement as soon as possible to take advantage of the power of compounding.

• Younger investors can afford to take more risks with their investments, while those closer to retirement should be more cautious.

• As retirement plans change over time, portfolios should be rebalanced, and estate plans should be modified as needed.

1. Understand Your Time Horizon

The primary foundation of a successful retirement strategy is laid by your current age and predicted retirement age. The more time you have between now and retirement, the more risk your portfolio can withstand. If you're young and have more than 30 years till retirement, you should invest most of your money in riskier investments like stocks. Stocks have typically outperformed other securities, such as bonds, over lengthy periods, although there will be volatility. The key word here is "long," which refers to at least ten years.

Furthermore, you'll need returns that outpace inflation to keep your purchasing power in retirement. "Inflation is like an acorn. It begins little, but with enough time, it can grow into a massive oak tree. Compound growth on our money is something we've all heard about, and it's something we all want. On the other hand, inflation is a form of 'compound anti-growth,' as it erodes the value of your money. Over 24 years, an low inflation rate of 3% will erode the value of your savings by 50%. It doesn't seem like much each year, but it adds up over time," says Chris Hammond, a Savannah, Tenn. financial advisor and founder of RetirementPlanningMadeEasy.com.

You might think saving a few bucks in your twenties doesn't mean much, but compounding will make it much more valuable by the time you need it.

Generally, as you get older, your portfolio should be more focused on income and capital preservation. This means putting more money into assets like bonds, which won't provide you the same returns as stocks but will be less volatile and provide you with the income you can live on. You'll be less concerned about inflation as well. A 64-year-old who plans to retire next year does not face the same worries about rising living costs as a much younger professional just starting in the field.

You should split your retirement strategy into several parts. Let's imagine a parent wants to retire in two years, pay for a child's education until they reach 18, and relocate to Florida. The investing strategy would be divided into three stages from building a retirement plan: two years until retirement (contributions are still made to the plan), saving and paying for college, and living in Florida (regular withdrawals to cover living expenses). To identify the best allocation approach, a multistage retirement plan must consider various time horizons and related liquidity needs. Your portfolio should also be rebalanced over time as your time horizon changes.

2. Determine Retirement Spending Needs

Having a reasonable expectation regarding post-retirement spending patterns will be easier to identify the required size of a retirement portfolio. Most people expect that their annual spending will amount to 70% to 80% of what it was before retirement. This assumption is frequently proven to be unrealistic, particularly if the mortgage is not paid off or unexpected medical expenditures arise. Retirees may also spend their first years after retirement splurging on travel or other bucket-list items.

"I feel that the ratio should be closer to 100 percent for retirees to have enough resources for retirement," says David G. Niggel, ChFC, CFP, AIF, president, founder, and CEO of Key Wealth Partners, LLC in Litiz, Pa. "The cost of living rises every year, particularly health-care costs. People are living longer and want to make the most of their retirement years. Retirees will require more income for a longer period; therefore, they must save and invest accordingly."

Because retirees are no longer required to work for eight hours or more per day, they have more leisure to travel, sightsee, shop, and partake in other expensive activities. More spending in the future necessitates extra savings today. Thus accurate retirement spending targets help in the planning process. "Your withdrawal rate is one of, if not the most important, factors in the longevity of your retirement portfolio. It's important to have an accurate estimate of your retirement costs because it will determine how much you withdraw every year and how you invest your account. Kevin Michels, CFP, EA, financial planner, and owner of Medicus Wealth Planning in Draper, Utah, argues that you might easily outlive your portfolio if you understate your spending. If you overstate your expenses, you risk not living the type of retirement lifestyle you want. When planning for retirement, it's also important to consider your longevity to don't outlive your savings. The average life span of individuals is increasing.

The longevity rates of individuals and couples (referred to as longevity risk) can be estimated using actuarial life tables.

Additionally, if you plan to buy a house or pay for your children's education after retirement, you may need more money than you anticipate. These expenses must be considered into the overall retirement strategy. Remember to review your plan at least once a year to ensure that you are on track with your savings. According to Alex Whitehouse, CRPC, CWS, AIF, president and CEO of Whitehouse Wealth Management in Vancouver, Wash., "early retirement planning accuracy can be improved by specifying and estimating early retirement activities, accounting for unexpected expenses in middle retirement, and forecasting what-if late-retirement medical costs."

3. Calculate the After-Tax Rate of Returns on Investments

After determining the expected time horizons and expenditure requirements, the real after-tax rate of return must be calculated to establish the portfolio's ability to generate the required income. A required rate of return of more than ten percent (before taxes) is usually unachievable, even for long-term investing. Because low-risk retirement portfolios generally comprise low-yielding fixed-income securities, this return criterion decreases as you become older.

Suppose an individual has a retirement portfolio worth $400,000 and income needs of $50,000, assuming no taxes and retaining the portfolio balance. In that case, they are relying on an exorbitant 12.5 percent return to get by. One of the key benefits of starting to plan for retirement at a young age is that the portfolio can be increased to provide a reasonable rate of return. The expected return on a $1 million gross retirement investing account would be a much more reasonable 5 percent.

Investment returns are usually taxed, depending on the type of retirement plan you have. As a result, the actual rate of return must be computed after taxes. However, determining your tax status when you start withdrawing funds is an important part of the retirement planning process.

4. Assess Risk Tolerance vs. Investment Goals

Whether you or a professional money manager is in charge of investment decisions is undoubtedly the most crucial stage in retirement planning. How much risk are you willing to accept to achieve your goals? Should a portion of one's income be invested in risk-free Treasury bonds to cover required expenses?

You must be comfortable with the risks you are taking in your portfolio and understand what is required and what is a luxury. Not only with your financial advisor but also with your family members, this is something that should be discussed seriously. Craig L. Israelsen, Ph.D., designer of 7Twelve Portfolio in Springville, Utah. "Don't be a micro-manager who reacts to daily market noise, "advises Craig L. Israelsen, Ph.D., designer of 7Twelve Portfolio in Springville, Utah. "Helicopter investors have a proclivity for over-managing their portfolios. When your portfolio's numerous mutual funds have a bad year, add extra money to them. It's like parenting: the child that needs your love the most often deserves it the least. Portfolios have a lot in common. Don't give up on the mutual fund you're upset with this year; it could be the best performer next year."

"Markets will go through long cycles of up and down, and if you're investing money you won't need for 40 years, you can afford to see your portfolio value grow and fall with those cycles," says John R. Frye, CFA, chief investment officer and co-founder of Crane Asset Management, LLC in Beverly Hills, Calif. "Buy, not sell, when the market falls. Refuse to succumb to fear. You'd want to buy clothes if they were on sale for 20% off, right? Why not stocks if they were 20% off?"

5. Stay on Top of Estate Planning

Another important step in a well-rounded retirement plan is estate planning, and each aspect necessitates the skills of different professionals in that industry, such as lawyers and accountants. Life insurance is also a key part of estate planning and retirement planning. Having a comprehensive estate plan and life insurance coverage ensures that your assets are distributed according to your wishes and that your loved ones will not experience financial hardship when you pass away. A well-thought-out plan can also help you avoid the costly and time-consuming probate process.

Another important aspect of estate planning process is tax planning. If a person chooses to leave assets to family or a charity, the tax implications of either gifting or passing the assets through the estate process must be compared.

A common retirement-plan investment strategy is to generate returns that cover yearly inflation-adjusted living expenses while maintaining the portfolio's value. The portfolio is then passed on to the deceased's beneficiaries. You should speak with a tax advisor to identify the best plan for the individual.

"Estate planning will vary over an investor's lifetime. Early on, matters such as powers of attorney and wills are necessary. When you start a family, you may find that trust is a vital part of your financial plan. Mark T. Hebner, president and founder of Index Fund Advisors, Inc. in Irvine, Calif., and author of "Index Funds: The 12-Step Recovery Program for Active Investors," believes that how you want your money dispensed later in life will be of the highest importance in terms of cost and taxes. "A fee-only estate planning attorney can help you prepare and maintain this aspect of your overall financial plan."

The burden of retirement planning is falling on individuals now more than ever. Few employees, especially in the private sector, can rely on an employer-provided defined-benefit pension. Switching to defined-contribution plans, such as 401(k)s, also implies that you, not your employer, will be in charge of investment management.

Striking a balance between reasonable return expectations and a desired level of living is one of the most difficult aspects of building a thorough retirement plan. Focus on building a flexible portfolio that can be modified regularly to reflect changing market conditions and retirement goals.

CHAPTER 5: BEST RV LOANS

Recreational vehicles, or RVs, are available in a number of types and price ranges. Many RV owners travel in comfort with these vehicles, but that comfort comes at a cost. RVs range in price from a few thousand dollars to well over a million dollars.

If you're considering purchasing an RV, you may require financing through an RV loan. However it's essential to understand that not all banks finance RVs; those that do often have loan limits and vehicle and borrower requirements.

To assist you in locating the finest RV loans, we examined over ten different lenders, taking into account factors such as interest rates, loan availability, maximum loan, payback periods, and even the type of vehicle financed. The following are our recommendations for the top RV loan lenders, along with a little explanation of why we chose each one.

Alliant Credit Union

You can borrow up to $300,000 for your RV purchase with Alliant Credit Union, and in many situations, same-day funding is available. Alliant's competitive interest rates and refinance options give it our overall #1 ranking for the finest RV loans.

Pros

Wide range of loan terms

Part- and full-timers accepted

Refinancing also offered

Same-day funding available

Cons

Online info is limited

Membership required

Alliant Credit Union is our top pick for recreational vehicle (RV) loans. It offers various competitive RV loan products for borrowers who intend to live in their vehicle on a part-time or full-time basis and provide speedy funding.

Though membership is required to apply for one of these loans, membership is easy: you must be an employee of (or retire from) one of Alliant's partner companies, have a family member who is already an Alliant member, live in specified communities, or be a member of certain partner organizations. If none of these apply to you, you can still join Alliant by just donating to Alliant's partner charity.

Alliant Credit Union offers RV loans to both part-time and full-time RVers. While many lenders will only lend to those who want to utilize their RV for leisure purposes, Alliant will finance those who intend to live in the vehicle full-time.

Loans of up to $300,000 are available with repayment durations of up to 20 years. Rates are competitive and range from 4.24 percent annual percentage rate to 5.24 percent annual percentage rate with an auto-pay discount. With an Alliant RV loan, there are no prepayment fees or penalties. Refinance loans are also available to qualified applicants, and borrowers in all 50 states can apply for both types of loans.

In many cases, same-day funding is possible, and loan pre-approval is available if you are still shopping around.

As a membership-based financial institution, Alliant does not post some information online. For example, they do not stipulate minimum down payments for RV loans or maximum loan-to-value (LTV) ratios for refinancing. Additionally, prospective borrowers are unable to shop for rates without first joining the credit union.

Southeast Financial's Credit Challenge Program is our top pick RV loans for those with subprime credit. This offers finance to those with a minimum credit score of 550 and those with previous bankruptcies.

Pros

Low-income requirements

Credit score minimum of only 550

Excellent consumer ratings

Previous bankruptcies are OK

Cons

Full-time and park model units not allowed

Financing is only available up to $75,000

Not a lender, but an aggregator

Prior positive installment loan history required

Obtaining a competitive loan can be difficult if you have low credit or a history of bankruptcy. However, Southeast Financial does not only accept borrowers with bad credit; they have an entire lending program dedicated to them.

Southeast Financial's Credit Challenge Program connects borrowers with credit scores as low as 550 to banks ready to grant them RV loans. Prior bankruptcies are permitted as long as they are discharged, and the minimum required consistent income is merely $20,000 to $30,000.

Collateralized recreational vehicles can be up to 15 years old, and loans up to $75,000 are available. Repayment terms range from 60 to 180 months, and there are no early repayment penalties. Loans are offered solely for recreational vehicles; however, this loan is not for you if you live in a motorhome or park model permanently.

Southeast Financial will review an applicant's prior installment loan history in order to match them with a loan package. This means that if you've never had an installment loan before—or if you defaulted on one—you may have difficulty getting approved (or snagging a lower rate). On that note, Southeast Financial does not publicize partner rates for non-prime loans, but does offer to cut your rate in the future if creditworthiness is established.

Southeast Financial now has a 4.4-star rating on TrustPilot, based on over 2,600 consumer reviews. The company also has an A+ rating with the Better Business Bureau.

BEST FOR GOOD CREDIT

Bank of the West

Bank of the West (through Essex Credit) offers affordable rates on loans up to $2 million for various recreational vehicles to applicants with a credit score of 700 or above.

Pros

Loans up to $2 million

Financing available to non-U.S. citizens

Repayment terms range from four to 20 years

Many different vehicle types allowed

Available in all 50 states

Rates as low as 3.59%*

Cons

Mileage maximums for used/refinanced RVs

No pre-approvals

Credit score of 700+ required

Park models not accepted

Loan fees apply

Bank of the West, formerly known as Essex Credit, was formed in 1874 in the United States. This bank offers customers in all 50 states incredibly competitive interest rates and various flexible RV loan packages, as long as they have a solid credit score (specifically, a score of 700 or higher). This lender offers rates as low as 3.99 percent annual percentage rate (APR) (up to 9.49 percent APR).

RV loans are available from $10,000 to $2 million through Bank of the West, with payback durations ranging from 48 to 240 months. Loans are also very inclusive, as they are available for a wide variety of different vehicles and uses.

For example, RV loans are available to part-time and full-time RVers, whereas many other lenders limit their lending to recreational vehicle owners. Loans are available for various recreational vehicles, including Class A/B/C motorhomes, travel trailers, fifth-wheels, pop-up campers, and truck campers. The only exceptions are park models and tiny homes.

Financing is available on new and used vehicles manufactured after 2012. The mileage limits are 60,000 for gasoline engines and 100,000 for diesel engines, regardless of whether you are purchasing secondhand or refinancing. Down payments range from 10% to 30%, depending on the purchase price, and additional expenses—such as taxes, warranties, warranties, and loan processing costs—can be rolled into the final loan, as long as the maximum loan-to-value ratio is reached.

Since Bank of the West's loan is collateral-based, pre-approvals aren't available. Loan approval can take one to two business days before you'll get a credit decision. Then, there is an extra wait time of 9 to 12 business days for RV loan applications to be processed—this is not the quickest lender available.

It is important to note that a loan from this bank comes with fees. Essex Credit does not charge application or prepayment fees but does charge loan processing fees.

BEST FOR QUICK FUNDING

LightStream

Our top recommendation for quick RV loans is LightStream, which can fund up to $100,000 the same day you apply.

Pros

No fees or prepayment penalties

Same-day funding available

Loans starting at just $5,000

Con

Repayment terms top out at 84 months

Low loan maximum

If you're looking for a low-interest RV loan with speedy approval, LightStream is your best option. This lender, which is a subsidiary of SunTrust, can fund your RV loan immediately upon application.

LightStream's loans begin at $5,000, allowing borrowers to purchase smaller, more affordable recreational vehicles than many other lenders allow. LightStream will lend up to $100,000, with repayment terms ranging from 24 to 84 months.

Interest rates range from 4.79 percent to 12.39 percent annual percentage rate, depending on the loan amount, creditworthiness of the borrower, and repayment term. A 0.50 percent auto-pay discount is available. There are no prepayment fees or penalties associated with a LightStream RV loan.

LightStream offers a Rate Beat Program, which offers a 0.10 percent lower interest rate than a rival lender if you want to save even more money. Certain conditions apply (for example, you must have been authorized for a loan with the same terms no more than one working day prior), but this is an excellent way for borrowers to snag in even lower rates.

BEST FOR LARGE LOANS

SunTrust

If you're considering purchasing a luxury camper with a higher price tag, SunTrust is our recommended lender. They offer loans up to $1.5 million at a competitive annual percentage rate and periods of up to 240 months.

Pros

Long repayment terms, if needed

Seven-figure loans offered

No points, processing fees, or service charges

Competitive, fixed APR

Cons

- The vehicle's title is held as collateral
- Not intended for the average RV purchase
- Sales/warranties tax cannot be rolled into the loan
- Not offered in all states

If you're considering purchasing a luxury recreational vehicle or motorhome, you'll need an RV loan with a significantly larger price tag. SunTrust motorhome loans are designed to provide financing for newer (10 years or less) luxury recreational vehicles with a starting price of $100,000 and a maximum loan amount of $1.5 million.

SunTrust, in contrast to some other high-loan lenders, does not post a minimum credit score criteria. They also waive loan processing fees, even on high-value loan products, which saves consumers money. There is a 15% to 20% down payment requirement, depending on the overall loan amount, and the title to your RV will serve as collateral.

SunTrust provides fixed interest rates ranging from 4.74 percent to 5.74 percent annual percentage rate on loans with repayment durations up to 240 months. However, there are no points, processing charges, service fees, and you can apply for a loan online in less than fifteen minutes.

You must keep in mind that neither a sales tax nor optional warranty expenses can be rolled into the loan. Loans are unavailable in Hawaii, Alaska, and Vermont, and SunTrust will only finance recreational RVs—so you cannot live in the motorhome full-time.

SunTrust is a conglomerate of numerous banks that have merged throughout the years (now under the Truist umbrella since its 2019 merger with BB&T). However, the bank's origins trace back to 1891.3 Truist now has an S&P financial strength grade of A-, with a stable outlook.

FAQs

What Is a Recreational Vehicle Loan?

A recreational vehicle loan is a type of loan used to fund the purchase of a recreational vehicle. RV loans are often available for motorhomes, travel trailers, fifth-wheels, pop-up campers, and in some cases, horse trailers.

Lenders may offer RV loans to various borrowers; some RV owners live in their RVs year-round, while others use them primarily for leisure purposes. To select the best lender, you must first determine how you intend to utilize your RV and then choose a lender that accepts those types of borrowers.

What Is the Difference Between RV and Car Loans?

While both RV and car loans provide finance for wheeled purchases, they have several distinctions. RV loans, for example, may cover trailer-style vehicles that lack an engine, such as fifth-wheel trailers.

RV loans also allow for significantly larger loans, which is important given the high cost of RVs. Certain RVs can cost well into the millions of dollars. Typically, you will not find an auto lender willing to provide that type of financing.

Finally, auto lenders are often unconcerned with how often you use your vehicle when approving you for a loan. On the other hand, RV lenders frequently disqualify some applicants based on their intended RV usage, whether part-time or full-time.

What Is a Good Credit Score for an RV Loan?

As with any loan product, the higher your credit score, the better the rate you will normally receive. To qualify for the most competitive RV loan rates, you should aim for a credit score of at least 700.

Naturally, several lenders offer RV loans to folks with poor credit as well. While certain income criteria and interest rates may apply, individuals with credit scores of 550 or higher are frequently approved for RV financing.

How Difficult Is It to Obtain an RV Loan Approval?

Obtaining approval for an RV loan is dependent on various factors, including the type of vehicle you wish to acquire and the frequency with which you intend to utilize it.

If you want to live in your RV full-time, it may be more difficult to locate a competitive lender than if you plan to use it part-time. Borrowers with 700+ credit scores will likewise have an easier (and faster) time obtaining funding.

Many lenders expect consistent income and may require income verification before loan approval. However, the real income amount required varies.

As with most financial instruments, borrowers must be at least 18 years old. Additionally, some lenders have higher age limits. Banks will normally require you to be a US citizen, while some lenders will finance purchases made by non-US citizens as long as they maintain a residence in the United States.

How We Selected the Best RV Loan, Providers?

We compared over ten different financial companies to compile this list of the finest RV loans and lenders. We evaluated their history, consumer evaluations, and availability, as well as the convenience with which consumers can apply for funding. We also examined loan repayment terms, credit score requirements, interest rates, loan minimums/maximums, and vehicle limitations to assist you in locating the best loan for your specific RV purchase.

CHAPTER 6: BEST STATES FOR FULL-TIME RV LIVING (2021)

With an average of 50 federal parks, the top states for full-time RV living have alternatives for every season and a diverse range of things to see and do. While you must choose a state to establish your domicile address while living in an RV full-time, it does not have to be the place where you spend most of your time. The ability to roam about is one of the best aspects of living in an RV, and our top 10 RV states should be on your list.

THINGS TO KEEP IN MIND

• The best states to live in if you're a full-time worker Living in an RV varies depending on the season, allowing you to follow the weather.

• If you seek a place to call home while traveling, Florida and Texas are good options.

• There are government parks and privately-run RV campgrounds in each of the top states to visit in your RV.

There's always something new to see in this vast country, whether you're just starting on a longtime ambition of full-time RV living or have been on the road for a while. For many, selecting the best states for full-time RV life is part of the journey, but if you're looking for a starting point, we've researched for you.

Because one of the best things about living in your RV full-time is that you can always keep an eye on the weather, our list includes states that are great to visit at any time of year. The states were graded based on weather, federal park access, and RV insurance alternatives.

In the frequently asked questions section, we'll go into the greatest places to live in an RV year-round, the state with the most RV owners, the cost of having a full-time RV home base, and RV-friendly states.

Keep in mind that you'll still need RV insurance, which differs from ordinary auto insurance in a few ways. Here you can locate the top auto insurance companies to meet your needs.

If you want to get a quote for your RV or automobile right away, just input your ZIP code into our online quote comparison tool. It will find you the best rates in your area based on your driving history and demographics.

We've also compiled a list of must-see national parks in each state so you can start that bucket list. There's something here for everyone who calls their RV home, whether they're looking for a state to spend a month or a year.

Top 10 States for Full-Time RV Living

You won't always be in the same place if you live in an RV full-time. While many full-timers spend months in one location, the majority have chosen a lifestyle that allows them to visit several locations throughout the year.

The finest places to live in an RV year-round are those with the warmest average temperatures, but we chose our favorites based on people who love to move around.

Every state is worth visiting at some point in your life on the road, but these top ten picks have some of the best parks, and each has a specific time of year when it's the best time to visit.

We selected them based on average temperatures, the number of federal parks in each state, and, of course, the number of RV insurance providers in each state.

While you may merely visit these locations, if you decide to make one of them your domicile (full-time RV permanent address), you'll need to know where to get affordable RV auto insurance. Below, we've highlighted which of these states are particularly good choices for establishing a domicile.

Are you ready to travel the road and see which states are the finest to call home – at least for a while? Let's get rolling.

#10 – Texas

Number of Federal Parks: 65

Must-See National Park: Big Bend National Park

Best Time to Visit: Spring

It's a large state with plenty to see and pleasant weather for most of the year. As a result, Texas is a popular destination for full-time RVers. If you're looking for a place to establish your domicile, Texas is one of the greatest options, thanks to its absence of income tax and simple access to mail-forwarding services. You should be aware, however, that Texas auto insurance premiums are on the higher side.

While you can choose from a variety of full-service RV parks in Texas, make sure you visit the state's lovely parks. Our top recommendation for a must-see is Big Bend, where desert visits and canyons carved by the Rio Grande offer a wide range of natural beauty. The best time to visit is in the spring because it is extremely hot in the summer and extremely cold in the winter.

#9 – Oregon

Number of Federal Parks: 48

Must-See National Park: Crater Lake National Park

Best Time to Visit: Late summer

Oregon has a diverse range of natural beauty, from the jagged coastline to the high desert and snow-capped mountains. It's also a fantastic area to improve your RV because there's no sales tax, and a strong camping culture means that those who live on the road are welcomed with open arms.

It's difficult to pick just one of Oregon's natural wonders to include on our must-see list, but Crater Lake National Park's crystal blue water edges out the competition. Oregon is notorious for its rainy weather, yet the driest and hottest months are late summer and early fall.

#8 – Arizona

Number of Federal Parks: 37

Must-See National Park: Grand Canyon National Park

Best Time to Visit: Spring

It's difficult to have an RV bucket list that doesn't include some time spent exploring the Grand Canyon. It is Arizona's most popular tourist destination and one of the country's most visited national parks.

Arizona has a lot more to offer full-time RVers than that. It's a terrific place to spend the winter months that are too cold up north, but you can also spend the spring here if the heat is too much for you in the summer. The weather is cooler in the state's northern region, and snow can be seen in the Grand Canyon.

Spring will provide you with the greatest combination of weather across the state.

#7 – North Dakota
Number of Federal Parks: 39

Must-See National Park: Theodore Roosevelt National Park
Best Time to Visit: Summer

North Dakota isn't ideal for living in an RV in the winter, but it's a fantastic destination to visit in the summer. It's a place to walk off the grid for a minute and breathe, with temperatures that aren't nearly as hot as the Southern states and expanses of wide, open space.

North Dakota may not come to mind when you think of breathtaking beauty, but Theodore Roosevelt National Park may convince you otherwise.

The park's Painted Canyon and awe-inspiring sunsets, as well as the chance to see bison roaming the countryside, are well worth the trip. It gives you a sense of how the area appeared hundreds of years ago.

#6 – Montana

Number of Federal Parks: 40

Must-See National Park: Glacier National Park

Best Time to Visit: Summer

Montana has something for everyone, from wide-open ranch terrain in the east to snow-capped peaks in the west. As they are in North Dakota, the winters are cold, but the summers offer lengthy days of moderate weather, making it an ideal site for full-time RVers who like to travel between the north and south.

Glacier National Park is hard to beat for pure beauty and magnificent mountain vistas. Some of the park's mountain roads aren't RV-friendly, so a "toad" (a car towed behind your RV) is an excellent alternative for getting to the park's farthest reaches. It's also an excellent starting place for a trip to the Canadian Rockies.

#5 – Florida

Number of Federal Parks: 41

Must-See National Park: Everglades National Park

Best Time to Visit: Late winter

Florida's warmth makes it a popular option for full-time RV life, but there's a better time to visit even in the Sunshine State. Avoid the spring break crowds by visiting Florida in the late winter, when the temperatures and humidity are still pleasant and hurricane season is still a few months away.

Everglades National Park, located at the very southern end of the state, is a must-see site. It's home to unique animals that can't be found anywhere else, and it's routinely one of the most popular parks in the country. Due to tax and mail-forwarding laws, Florida is an excellent choice for establishing your domicile, just like Texas.

Bear in mind, though, that Florida auto insurance is on the high side.

#4 – New York

Number of National Parks: 43

Must-See National Park: Niagara Falls National Heritage Area

Best Time to Visit: Early fall

While some will argue that the best time to visit New York is in the spring, and others will argue that the best time to visit is during the Christmas season, the best time to visit this state for a full-time RVer is in the fall. Winter is a little too cold for RV living, while spring tends to be rainy. On the other hand, Fall brings with it a spectacular display of foliage that is well-known around the country.

Fall will help you avoid the honeymoon crowds, especially if your plans take you to upstate New York to see Niagara Falls. If you do decide to visit the Big Apple, you'll be surprised to learn that there are a surprising number of RV sites with easy access.

Stay a little further out and take public transportation if you don't want to sit in traffic.

#3 – Washington State

Number of Federal Parks: 46

Must-See National Park: Olympic National Park

Best Time to Visit: Summer and early fall

Washington State, like Oregon, is known for a lot of rain, especially along the coast. It does, however, have beautiful summers that last well into the fall, just like Oregon. It's one of the few spots on the mainland where you can hike on an active volcano.

The coast is well-known, and Olympic National Park offers everything from mountains to tide pools to visitors.

Washington State has no income tax, making it a viable alternative for those seeking a domicile state.

If you use a domicile address in Washington for your RV, your auto insurance rates will be reduced as well. It's a terrific site for full-time RVers to spend the shoulder season before heading south for the winter.

#2 – Virginia

Number of Federal Parks: 48

Must-See National Park: Shenandoah National Park

Best Time to Visit: Spring through fall

Summers in Virginia can be hot, although not quite as hot as places further south. Even though winter isn't the best time to visit, you won't get frostbite. The temperatures are pleasant in an RV most of the year. There are also plenty of sights to view as well. Virginia's landscape boasts a lot of variety, ranging from huge beaches to lakes surrounded by green peaks, making it an excellent area to call home for a few months and take a break from the road.

#1 – California

Number of Federal Parks: 91

Must-See National Park: Yosemite National Park

Best Time to Visit: All year

Because California is so large and diverse, you could spend a whole year here in your RV and yet not see everything. California has a seemingly endless array of options, from the peaks of the Sierra Nevadas to the famous beaches of Los Angeles County.

Because you're taking your home with you, you may stay here for a while without having to worry about the state's exorbitant housing costs.

Yosemite National Park is the most visited country, and some portions of the park require reservations just to see. Reservations at one of the many nearby parks - made well in advance, are required if you wish to bring your RV here. However, while you wait, there are plenty of other things to do in California.

Enter your ZIP code to see companies that offer low-cost auto insurance.

Full Study Results: All States Ranked for Full-Time RV Living

If you've opted to live in an RV full-time, you're probably eager to see as much of the world as possible. We ranked each state based on the average temperature, the number of federal parks, and the number of RV insurance companies available. The rankings for each state are shown on the map below.

You'll note that Alaska is ranked 11th, following the top 10. While it's a beautiful destination to see and visit, it's important to note that traveling there in an RV is no easy task. The relatively perilous Alaska Highway (also known as the Alcan Highway), which is best navigated during the summer months, is not included in our ranking criteria.

Frequently Asked Questions: RV Living and Costs

Living full-time in an RV can be a fantastic experience, but it can also be challenging. Below are some of the most frequently asked questions concerning RVing.

#1 – What states allow full-time RV living?

You can live in an RV full-time in any state as long as you park it in an area where it's allowed. This is when things can get a little tricky.

The question of what states allow you to reside in an RV on your property is a different one entirely. You'll have to follow city and county laws, some of which prohibit RVs from being used as permanent houses.

So, is it illegal to live full-time in an RV? Some restrictions govern where you may park your RV and for how long and how many people can dwell in a certain amount of space. Of course, there's a difference between living in an RV on your own or someone else's land for the entire year and taking your RV on the road all year.

#2 – What is the best RV to live in full time?

Most full-time RVers prefer larger models, but it's truly a matter of personal preference and budget. Slide-out RVs provide additional living space, and larger tanks mean fewer dumping stations are required.

#3 – If you live in an RV, what is your address?

People who live in RVs are required to set up a domicile address. That's your permanent legal address, which you use to receive mail and for things like your full-time RV driver's license, taxes, and RV registration.

You should also keep in mind that you cannot have auto insurance from a state other than where you live. So, your domicile state is also where you are insured.

There are a few states that make this process easier than others. What state is the best for RV registration?

The ideal state for registering an RV and establishing a domicile depends on your preferences. Still, Texas, Florida, and South Dakota are all popular choices thanks to easing mail forwarding and the lack of income tax.

Keep in mind that the law theoretically requires you to spend at least a portion of the year in the state where you reside. So, when deciding between Texas and South Dakota as a domicile, think about where you'd rather spend your time.

#4 – Which state is most suitable for full-time RVers?

According to our research, Washington State (3), Virginia (2), and California (1) are the three finest states for full-time RV life. They all have at least 46 federal parks (California has 91) and enjoy pleasant weather and spectacular scenery.

#5 – What states can you live in an RV full time?

Most states allow you to live in an RV full-time, but some are better than others. Weather, federal parks, national parks, the number of RV campgrounds, and the expense of living are just a few of the considerations for RV owners when deciding where to live full-time.

#6 – Where do full-time RVers stay?

RV parks are popular with full-time RVers because they provide a sense of community and allow them to meet new people. They also often have the necessary infrastructure for full-time RV living.

#7 – What RVs are rated for a full-time living?

Because RVs come in a variety of styles and sizes, their prices can range in the thousands. Buying one depends on your budget as well as the level of comfort you require.

#8 – What state has the most RV owners?

Florida is one of the most popular places for RV owners, Because of the pleasant weather all year and the absence of a state income tax.

#9 – Is it cheaper to live on a boat or RV?

RVs are often less expensive than boats because the lowest price point is a trailer that you can pull behind you rather than a residence on wheels. In general, they don't have any special licensing requirements.

#10 – How much does it cost to live in an RV park per month?

Staying in an RV park will cost you between $500 and $1,200 per month. A lot depends on the park, its location, and the number of amenities available.

#11 – What is the best RV for the money?

If you have the money, RVshare.com recommends the Newmar Dutch Star. While it is a luxurious RV, the company allows you to personalize the interior decor and the RV in numerous ways to meet your demands.

CHAPTER 7: TIPS TO SAVE A LOT OF MONEY AND LIVE COMFORTABLY

It takes time to achieve long-term financial success. Investments require time to accumulate, compound interest takes time to work, and job decisions take time to pay off.

The issue is that when you're in the middle of a financial crisis, you usually don't have much time. Bills continue to pile up. Debtors are contacting you. You've just been slammed with a huge bill. You must make drastic financial changes, and you must do so quickly.

Frugality is essential in these situations. What you require are effective techniques to reduce your expenses without sacrificing your quality of life. Choose one of these tips and apply it to your life where it makes sense to reduce your spending to have the funds to pay your debts and stabilize your finances.

50 ways to save money fast

1. Make a list before you go shopping. Make a list of things you want to buy before going into a store for any reason. A shopping list will help focus there, but it's also useful at niche stores like bookstores and apparel stores. Do some research on sales or which items to buy before you enter.

2. Find a better bank. Your bank should ideally offer no-fee checking, a large ATM network, and excellent internet banking services if your current one charges your account maintenance fees or ATM fees regularly. Are several excellent full-service banks that provide these services and some excellent online-only banks that excel at online banking.

3. Turn the television off. Television consumes electricity, generally involves a fee, and is replete with commercials, even inside the shows

themselves (product placement). Consider watching less television and substituting something else.

4. Stop collecting and start selling. Rather than accumulating more belongings (and thus having less time and energy to devote to each one), aim for a small number of truly loved and used possessions. Start by selling some of your non-essential items.

5. Enroll in free consumer rewards programs. If you are already shopping at a store, see if they have a free customer rewards program and sign up if they do. Create a new email address, especially for these rewards programs, so that your regular email isn't flooded with offers, and then check that email if you're thinking about buying something. These programs often result in discounts and rewards on items you are already going to buy.

6. Pay off your rewards credit card in full each month. If you use a credit card, make it a habit to pay off your balance in full each month. This ensures you aren't charged finance fees or interest once you've established that habit; concentrate on using a rewards credit card that corresponds to your spending habits so that the rewards are only beneficial to you.

7. Master the 30-day rule. The 30-day rule states that you should wait 30 days before making a large purchase (say, anything above $20) that isn't necessary. Put that item on your wishlist and come back to it in 30 days. Go for it if you still want it! If you decide you don't want it anymore, you'll have saved a lot of money on something you didn't even want! This is a fantastic strategy to avoid bad purchasing impulses.

8. Master the 10-second rule, too. The 10-second rule advises that before making any purchase, think for 10 seconds about why you shouldn't buy it. Is it truly necessary? Do you already have something like that? Is it possible to borrow something similar? If you start to have doubts, simply put the items down. You can always get it some other time!

9. Invite friends over. There's a great want to go somewhere for social activities, but going somewhere typically means spending money only to enjoy the company of others. Instead, mix it up sometimes and have

some pals over. Have a movie night with your family at home. Take a page from strategy #74 and have a low-budget dinner party.

10. Make repairs to your outfit. You can fix several minor clothing issues with a little thread and a needle. Instead of dumping a shirt with a fraying seam or missing button, do the simple repair yourself and extend the garment's life.

11. Do not overspend on entertaining your kids. This is particularly true for younger children, but it also happens to older ones. Children primarily desire time rather than material possessions. Of course, if you ask them for something, they'll come up with a list, but what they want is time with you.

12. Pay off your credit cards. Avoid putting more money on your credit cards until they're completely paid off. Every transaction you make on a credit card pushes the balance in the wrong direction, increasing the amount of interest you'll have to pay. Learn to survive solely on the funds in your bank account.

13. Negotiate rates with your credit card company. If you have a credit card balance, talk to your credit card company about lowering your interest rate.

14. Take advantage of a zero-interest credit card balance transfer. If #13 doesn't work for you, seek a balance transfer offer with no interest. This will allow you to transfer your balance to a new card and pay no interest for a period, usually 12 or 18 months. When you pay it off, all of your money goes toward reducing the debt rather than vanishing in form in interest payments.

15. Go through your closets and clean them out. Take everything out of your closets and storage areas, decide what you want to keep, and then put it back. Everything that is still in the closet needs to be sold. Take that money and use it to pay your debt.

16. Drink more water and less soda and juice. Water is a remarkably low-cost commodity. Juice and soda are more expensive. Furthermore, soda and juice can have long-term health consequences.

17. Stay away from fast food. Fast food is convenient, and it may appear to be a good deal at times, but it is not a good deal in terms of calories. If you want a quick and much cheaper snack option when you are out and about, buy a box of granola bars and put some in your car.

18. Give up smoking and limit your alcohol consumption. Tobacco, alcohol, and other vices all damage your long-term health while also costing you money. Get rid of those bad habits!

19. Save soups and casseroles. Make additional batches of soups or casseroles and freeze the surplus for an easy and quick meal when you're short on time.

20. Make use of the library. While the library does lend out free books, did you know that many libraries also lend out DVDs and Blu-rays, as well as tools and other equipment? Furthermore, libraries offer complimentary groups, seminars, and other events.

21. Switch off all lights. Every 13 hours, a 75-watt lightbulb consumes approximately one kilowatt-hour of energy. You pay $0.13 for a kilowatt-hour of energy. Thus, if many bulbs are left on for an extended period, the cost accumulates. The solution is twofold: Turn off lights when leaving rooms and replace incandescent bulbs with energy-efficient LED bulbs that provide similar lighting at a fraction of the cost.

22. Lower your thermostat. Rather than setting your thermostat to "absolutely comfortable," aim for a slightly cooler temperature in the winter and a slightly warmer temperature in the summer. Wear a sweatshirt in the winter, and take off your shoes and socks in the summer.

23. Open the windows; rather than relying on energy to maintain a comfortable temperature in your home, open the windows and turn on the ceiling fans. This will consume significantly less energy than your air conditioner or furnace. Use them only during the most intense weather conditions, when open windows and fans are insufficient.

24. Run your ceiling fans in the correct direction. There are several excellent energy-saving ceiling fan methods, but this one is probably the finest. Here is a small switch that controls the direction in which the

blades turn. In the winter, you want the blades to spin clockwise when you look up at them. In the summer, you want them to spin in the opposite direction. This keeps warm air in the room during winter and cool air during summer.

25. Buy appliances based on reliability. Reliability should be the primary consideration if you want to get the most for your money when purchasing household appliances. Consumer Reports is a good resource for reliability data, and you should stay with models and manufacturers with high-reliability ratings for the type of appliance you're purchasing. When you purchase a 15-year appliance instead of a 10-year appliance, you purchase only two of them over 30 years instead of three.

26. Use the grocery store flyer. This is the fundamental strategy for effectively low-cost meal planning for busy families. Each week, get your preferred grocery store's weekly flyer, choose some on-sale ingredients, and create a meal plan around them. Then, using that plan as a guide, create your grocery list.

27. Switch to your local discount grocery store. Compare local grocers' prices by purchasing a week's worth of groceries from each and comparing prices on common items. Start shopping at the store with the lowest average price.

28. Don't browse at stores for entertainment. While many people engage in "retail therapy," it amplifies financial problems, not alleviates them. Other strategies to entertain and de-stress include going on hikes or planning uninterrupted time for hobbies.

29. Choose a hobby that involves making things. Reduce your reliance on activities that revolve around collecting and consuming things and increase your dependence on hobbies that require doing or making things. Baking, cooking, knitting, crocheting, and making fermented foods are examples of hobbies that center around making easy and affordable things to start.

30. Make a maintenance schedule. An auto, home, and appliance maintenance checklist is a comprehensive list of all ongoing maintenance tasks. Once a month, go through the list and take care of

everything due. This increases the life of your automobiles and appliances and makes costly home repairs much less frequent.

31. Cancel unused subscriptions and memberships. Any magazines that you aren't reading? Do you have unused gym or other club memberships? What about subscription-based streaming services? Cancel them! Examine your bank and credit card statements to ensure you haven't missed anything!

32. Look for a used option first. Whenever you are considering purchasing something nonperishable, seek a secondhand option first. While this method is not always ideal, it works for various items, from musical instruments and sporting goods to small household appliances and clothes.

Make it a habit to shop secondhand first for everything from tea cups to T-shirts, and you'll often find what you're searching for at a significant discount.

33. Shop around for a new insurance package. Homeowners and auto insurance are always major expenses. There is a lot of money to be saved by shopping around and getting switching discounts.

34. Remove your credit card numbers from your online accounts. While keeping your credit card details in an online account may seem easy, it is a temptation. It's quite easy to tap a couple of times and make a purchase.

35. Do holiday shopping right after holidays. Following a holiday, many stores offer steep discounts on decorations and other holiday-related items. Buy Christmas paper and lights immediately after Christmas. Purchase creepy Halloween items immediately after Halloween. Buy egg dyeing kits immediately following Easter. Then simply store them until next year.

36. Join a volunteer program. Spending your leisure time doing volunteer work means that you're not only doing things for free, but you're also likely to pick up some important skills along the way. For instance, a day spent working on a Habitat for Humanity house is a free day of activity that also teaches you some useful carpentry skills.

37. Try generic or store brand versions of items. Rather than purchasing the familiar name brand version of everything, give the store brand version a try. You will often discover that store brands work and you'll save going forward.

38. Switch to term life insurance. Term life insurance protects your family in the event of your untimely death.

39. Prepare as many meals at home as possible. Cooking at home is, as always, less expensive than dining out. The disadvantage, of course, is the effort and expertise required. The idea is to ease yourself into cooking by preparing simple, affordable, yet delectable meals at first until you have the necessary kitchen skills.

40. Buy cars based on reliability and fuel efficiency. When shopping for a car, prioritize reliability and fuel efficiency. Reliability means fewer repairs and longer life, especially if you adhere to the recommended maintenance schedule, while fuel efficiency means fewer stops at the gas pump.

41. Swap babysitting with your neighbors. If you have little children babysitting is an ongoing expense. One good solution is to speak with the parents of your children's friends and arrange for regular babysitting swaps, which will provide you and your partner with a free date night.

42. Learn to jazz up leftovers. Almost all leftovers are useful. Many meals can be reheated directly, but what about leftovers?

43. Cut down your wardrobe. This is not to say that you should discard everything you no longer wear. Instead, put most of your wardrobe into storage and wear a subset of your clothing until it begins to wear out, then "shop" for replacements in storage. This way, you can avoid purchasing clothes for a long time.

44. "Brown bag" your lunch. B ring your food instead of eating lunch with coworkers. Encourage your coworkers to do the same thing so that you can share meals and enjoy the camaraderie.

45. Try making repairs yourself. Try to make repairs yourself instead of calling a repair person. Start by searching YouTube for a video on how to resolve the issue and, if it appears feasible, give it a try. Many minor

fixes are relatively simple, such as fixing most plugged toilets or handling a leaky faucet.

46. Get in the habit of taking notes on your phone. You have a great idea for saving money or anything else you want to remember; jot it a note on your phone. Then, once or twice a day, review it. This will prevent you from forgetting about good bargains or money-saving ideas.

47. Move to a lower cost-of-living area. If you can find work in a different area, make the deliberate choice to relocate to one with a cheaper cost of living, particularly if you can maintain your salary. This is an excellent option for those who work remotely.

48. Look for free events. Check your city's website and any free local newspapers. Both are excellent resources for finding free events in your town: community festivals, business grand openings, and free concerts.

49. Properly inflate your car tires. Underinflated tires create more friction with the road, resulting in faster wear on tires and worse fuel efficiency. Check the air pressure in your tires once a month and fill them to the appropriate maximum pressure.

50. Ride a bicycle. Want to save money on transportation? Use a bicycle for your commute or, if your bike has detachable bags, use it for simple errands such as grocery shopping.

CHAPTER 8: 20 WAYS TO MAKE MONEY WHILE FULL-TIME RVING

- START YOUR OWN BUSINESS

If you're anything like me, you'll frequently get sick and tired of the boss man constantly on your back. Does the company you work with grate on your nerves to the extent where you'd love to scream for some relief? Did they give you the bonus they promised or that well-earned pay increase? If this seems all too familiar, you might want to consider other possible career paths. Nowadays, big enterprises aren't the only option. Over the last decade, the times have changed. Recently it has become much more feasible to go it alone and make money for yourself, particularly thanks to the rise of the internet. I bet such a career move has been sitting in the back of your mind for some time. It's only natural. We all ponder things like that from time to time. I understand this can be a daunting prospect, but isn't the possibility of losing your job whenever cutbacks have to be made just as scary?

Many people choose to strike out on their own, and you may do the same. The independence you receive, in my opinion, is the most tempting feature. Let's face it: when you start your own business, you are the boss, and you choose the rules. No one likes to be told what to do - it's in our nature. However, when you start your own business, there's more than being in charge of yourself; there is a lot to do with your actual income. Everyone knows that you work within a machine when working for a large company, ultimately making money for someone else. And no one likes being a dispensible cog. This inevitably means the boss is making a mint while you live on pennies. And surely you'll agree that's no way to live. It's about time you thought of starting your own business and put in some serious graft. It's always a good idea to start slowly and on a small scale. You can keep your current job and work with your business on the side, building up your business gradually. You can get rid of the boss and the problems that come with it once it's up and going. Believe me when I say that this happens more frequently than you might believe.

If you're looking for a unique way to start your own business, consider using the internet as a resource or a marketplace. You can find a variety of free material on the internet to help you get started. The Internet is a terrific marketing and selling tool, and it is unquestionably a valuable resource in today's business world. Consider the possibilities of a worldwide market. So if you are looking to start your own business, it's time to get down to the hard work and research. Get yourself online and start enjoying your life doing what you want to do for your end.

Anyone can go it alone. You don't need to be qualified, although you do need a good idea and the drive and determination to work at something. So, if you want to make it a success go for it - start your own business today!

- WORK IN A NATIONAL PARK

All across America, there are many beautiful national parks, and each of them needs to be staffed with those willing to take on the challenges that national park jobs bring. These parks are filled with so much wonder and excitement that they draw tens of thousands of visitors every year. If you are looking for a national park job, then this is good news for you.

Working in one of many available national parks is a great way to live and work in pure splendor. The great part about finding park jobs is that there are many to be had on a seasonal and permanent basis. That means that you can decide whether you want to find a park job that is only for part of the year, like a summer job in Yellowstone, or you can find a job that will last all year round, such as working to preserve part of a national park's habitat.

You can also choose your beauty. With parks in many parts of the country, you can decide to opt for the mountains or even the flats of the country. If you decide to work a seasonal park job, you could effectively take a couple of different jobs throughout the year and see what area and job are best. This also allows you to see different parts of the country while still making a living.

National park jobs are numerous, and people of all skill levels often find jobs at parks. While many think park jobs are reserved for a park ranger, many other positions need to be filled to keep America's parks running smoothly. Jobs in lodging, recreational, and even retail are all available at the national parks across the United States. While it may not appear so, many personnel must staff a national park, particularly the larger ones, effectively.

The fact that many park jobs are outside occupations is maybe the finest aspect. What a fantastic method to make a living. You not only get paid every week, but you also get to breathe in all that fresh air and enjoy all that America's great national parks have to offer.

If you enjoy being outside and meeting new people, there are various occupations available that may be ideal for you. Everyone has to work, but there is no saying that you can't enjoy what you do while you work and live-in pure beauty with a job at one of our nation's parks. So, if you are up for the challenge, then get out there, explore your career opportunities, explore your future growth, and most importantly, explore yourself with a national park job.

- ONLINE TEACHING

There are many jobs considered to be the best employment for people. One of them is online teaching. Online teaching has changed the face of the tutorial since as far as the past decade. These methods are in the form of an actual group tutorial class or home school methods in the old days. However, since the advent of internet progress, the tutorial has been made easier and more convenient through the internet and its software programs. AS far as education is concerned, online teaching is considered the best job in the world, and here are the reasons why?

I. No pressure

Every instructor must face their students and maintain an authoritative, confident, and precise demeanor. Educators are held to this standard by educational institutions. However, in online teaching, you don't have to place as much emphasis on these factors. In general, online instruction does not necessitate the same level of rigor as traditional teaching. Why? It's because online teaching does not always necessitate the acquisition of a license. You can teach at your discretion as long as the organization believes you can make someone understand. "Can I establish friends with online students?" you might wonder. The question "Why not?" is frequently posed by tutorial institutes. However, in online teaching, the response is already implied: "You must!"

II. No stage fright

Stage fright is a common phobia for people. Every performer always has it. With online teaching, you can easily ward that stage fright because you do not have to deal with them in person. Only a webcam or a voice microphone can make it possible for some companies who do not strictly impose the rule of having a webcam, all the better. You can talk to the student without seeing you slouching on your chair or making faces when you are furious about their inability to learn.

III. Home-based

Since online jobs are done on the internet, and most online jobs are home-based, the same goes for online teaching. Thus they say, "Home is where the heart is." Or more like saying, "There is no place like home." It is the same thing with online teaching. It is one of the things that made it considered to be one of the fulfilling occupations online. Eliminating the idea of traveling cost is the greatest point you can consider. No costs paid for transportation or even if you have a car of your own, there is no time wasted for traveling. Even if one lives far from the job, there is no need to worry about working late. It does not guarantee that you will never be chastised for tardiness by corporate officials. You may still be late if you did not log in on time. You are, nevertheless, in your element. Everything becomes easier as a result.

- REMOTE WORK

One of the numerous inquiries I get from business owners is how to work productively when they are not in the office, i.e., working remotely. With so many technology options accessible today, determining which one(s) are the most effective can be difficult.

I have a dedicated office space in my house with a desktop PC and wireless all-in-one printer, the standard solo service professional office setup. Yet, there are times when I don't want or can't be at work but still have to work. I've been traveling a lot for work lately, but I still want to stay in touch with my clients and business. And sometimes I need a change of scenery, especially now that the weather is starting to warm up and it's good to work from my laptop outside.

So now I'd want to share with you my top five remote working tools, which allow me to work outside of my workplace while still having access to all of my "things" as if I were there.

1. Gmail - I'm a die-hard Outlook user who despises the Gmail interface; yet, when I'm not in the office but still require access to my emails and schedule, Gmail is a terrific option. When I am on vacation, I forward all of my emails to my Gmail account. I recently discovered a useful tool that syncs my Outlook calendar with my Gmail calendar, ensuring that I always have the most up-to-date version of my itinerary. I can also use my Droid smartphone to access my Gmail email and calendar, which is another wonderful method for me to keep connected and on top of my schedule.

2. Dropbox - If you haven't heard of Dropbox, it's a terrific way to share data between your desktop PC and your laptop without having to copy things from your PC to a flash drive and then back to your laptop. The Dropbox software creates a new folder on your PC/laptop that you can drop your files into and access from any computer with the Dropbox software installed. You can also access your files by logging into your account on the internet.

This service is also used by my clients so that they have access to all of their files.

3. TeamViewer - I owe this useful piece of software to my hubby! This enables me to access my desktop PC from any other computer as if I

were sitting in front of it. For example, if I want to work on the deck, I take my laptop with me and use TeamViewer to connect it to my desktop, and I can access EVERYTHING as if I were sitting at my desk.

4. Skype - my 'office' number has been a SkypeIn number for years. This means I can forward this number to my cell phone or install Skype's software on my laptop and make and receive calls just like I was sitting at my workplace.

5. MiFi - a MiFi is a mobile wireless router offered by your cell phone carrier that allows you to connect to the Internet from anywhere with a cell phone signal if you're traveling and are in an area without Internet access.

You can now operate your business practically anywhere because you have all of these tools to facilitate effective and profitable remote working.

- VIRTUAL ASSISTANT

Described, a virtual assistant assists business owners with administrative tasks but does not necessarily do these tasks in the owner's office. This is what distinguishes us as "virtual." Although some virtual assistants spend time at their customers' workplaces, the majority do not.

Most virtual assistants deal with a diverse range of clients from all over the county or worldwide. Because the work is virtual, the options for location are virtually infinite.

Virtual assistants also charge for their work on an hourly basis. Every virtual assistance business is different in that they may have hourly packages setup or retainer rates but most charge a flat hourly rate for their services. The clients then pay the virtual assistant for the work they perform for them in a given pay period. The virtual assistant also defines these pay periods.

Most virtual assistants work from home and have their home office setup. This allows flexibility in the hours that you would work, and it also allows you the comfort of working in your home.

There are various types of virtual assistants. Most virtual assistants focus on the administrative aspects of assistance and provide services such as word processing, editing, proofreading, document creation, scheduling, event management, file organization, and other similar tasks. These virtual assistants generally charge in the $15 to $25 range per hour.

The next type of virtual assistant would be what I call the 'web savvy' virtual assistant who does administrative-based support and has experience in the operations required to run an online business. The tasks included here include shopping cart setup and maintenance, website maintenance, autoresponder management, blog posting, etc. These virtual assistants can charge a bit more since their knowledge is at a higher expertise level than the administrative-based virtual assistant. These virtual assistants generally charge between $20 and $40 per hour.

The last type of virtual assistant would be someone who considers themselves more of an online business manager. This person would work with their clients in a business partner role and provide a mutually beneficial relationship. What I mean by this is that this type of virtual assistant would be much more inclined to evaluate the operations of a client's business and suggest ways in which they could improve their processes. These virtual assistants generally charge $50 and above per hour.

The types of skills you would need to be a virtual assistant depend on what type of virtual assistant you are looking to become. At the very least, one must be knowledgeable with the office-based software programs - Word, Excel, PowerPoint, Outlook, etc. - and the Internet. You must be able to have general knowledge of these things before you can begin to serve your clients, or you will cause frustration to both yourself and your client.

- TRAVELING MEDICAL PROFESSIONAL

With today's heightened knowledge and love for travel, a new breed of professionals has evolved to capitalize on the trend, whether it's for official business or a much-needed vacation. Regardless of their professions, businessmen, consultants, lawyers, and medical professionals are among them.

Yes, you read that correctly. Medical professionals travel a lot as well! The majority of their trips are for work-related reasons, such as attending medical conferences or conducting research.

However, due to their busy schedules and many things on their minds, medical professionals will occasionally encounter problems or inconveniences resulting from their travels. So, here are a few pointers to help medical professionals have a productive and enjoyable trip.

Bring some basic medical supplies (it might come in handy)

As if their wonderful work within the four walls of a clinic or hospital isn't enough, medical professionals will never stop saving lives. It may happen while you're on your trip this time. That is why, whenever they are out of town, it is always best to have the fundamental instruments they require to practice their trade.

Basic Survival Suggestions

Despite being the reason for patients' lives, doctors require assistance in surviving in a foreign environment. They should make photocopies of their credit cards (front and back) and jot down their credit card companies and bank's contact information. It's wise not to keep all of your valuables and cash in the same location.

Get a premium service, such as a boutique travel concierge.

Traveling may be incredibly stressful, which is why some of these excursions are referred to as "getaways." You'll have to cope with various languages, cultures, and currencies, as well as logistical headaches. Using the services of a boutique travel concierge would be advantageous if you desire high-quality service and accommodations.

Make sure all of your travel documentation are up to date.

In the long run, medical practitioners would benefit from learning the phone numbers of the country's embassy. They can also photocopy their passports and other important documents. Always pack these essentials in carry-on luggage to minimize problems if your other bags go missing in transit.

Traveling can be difficult for anyone, even experienced medical professionals.

- FREELANCE WRITER (REPORTER, BLOG POST FOR HIRE, TECHNICAL WRITING, BUSINESS WRITING, EDITING)

When people need help creating or updating the material on their website or blog, they turn to freelance writers for hire. The finest freelance writers are usually willing to write about any subject that their clients require, no matter how technical, scientific, or thorough it is. There are freelance writers available for multilingual people and can translate text into the client's preferred language.

Good freelancers can also meet a client's deadline because it demonstrates that they value their job and respect their wishes. Their clients trust their abilities and think that they will deliver great results as a result of their professionalism. It's also crucial to find a freelance writer who can produce new, original content on any topic. Some people prefer looking for freelance writers for hire in magazines and newspapers because they trust the quality of their work, depending on the project's sensitivity.

Freelance writers come in a variety of shapes and sizes. Some of them work full-time as authors, while others work part-time to accommodate their schedules. There are freelance writers available for hire who write on specific themes based on the needs of their clients. Most of the time, these writers chose topics about which they are well-versed. They primarily write about travel, food, medicine, and other related topics. Freelancers who create articles can attract the attention of readers by using very clean and expressive language. Articles are popular among freelancers since they may be found on the Internet and in newspapers and magazines.

Executives and managers pay freelancers to write for their periodicals and keep their websites up to date with new and enhanced items. Because of the fierce competition and marketing in the business world, these freelancers are usually qualified and knowledgeable in business and discuss the company's services and products.

Newspaper and magazine proprietors hire freelance columnists to write about and comment on the current market and national trends. Depending on the assignment, they must write about an observation or a topic of interest once a week or once a month. Copywriters are freelance writers who sell a company's products and ensure that the website receives consistent traffic.

Because there are always new items and services to sell, copywriting is one of the most common writing tasks for freelancers. The top freelance writers for hire can write with zeal and zeal that people are compelled to try the product or service. Copywriting is one of the highest-paying freelance writing jobs.

Freelancers that specialize in writing grants for clients are also available. This clientele is frequently on the lookout for government and other institution awards. These writers are tasked with appealing to these institutions and ensuring that their customers receive a favorable answer. As a result, clients looking for these freelancers ensure that they have relevant experience.

- WEB DESIGNER

There are many distinct forms of web design, ranging from simple content managed and e-commerce web designs like those used by Amazon, eBay, and Tesco to complicated content managed and e-commerce web designs like those used by huge brand names like Amazon, eBay, and Tesco. Some businesses, even some well-known ones, have unprofessional-looking and poorly built websites. Some websites appear fantastic, but because of the high graphical content and low text, they can take a long time to load, aren't user-friendly, and don't give what the visitor is searching for.

A well-designed website

While many parts of website design vary from one to the next, many things are consistent throughout most websites on the internet. The navigation, or menu, is the most noticeable feature. The way a website's menu functions and appears is crucial. Visitors to a website look for certain characteristics that will determine whether they stay and interact or depart. Stickiness is a term used to describe a website's capacity to keep visitors intrigued. Visitors desire an appealing, visually stimulating experience, but possibly even more vital, 'ease of use.' For websites that want their users to stay, make an inquiry, and eventually complete a transaction and acquire a product or service, website usability is critical.

Web Design That Is Simple To Use

Because they do not want to learn how to use a website every time they locate a new one, internet users choose easy-to-use websites. They shouldn't be able to use a website after only a few seconds of browsing the homepage; else, they'll abandon it and go elsewhere. Because quick user interaction is critical, having a fast-loading website is also necessary for a website's success. Internet customers do not want to wait, even with faster internet connections such as broadband.

Imagine going to a store on the high street and being ignored for 5 minutes by the shop employees at the counter, even though you have made it plain that you require assistance. There's a link here between how an internet user feels when they visit a website that's badly designed, difficult to use, hostile, and slow to load. A website's success depends on whether it was well-thought-out and created with the user in mind. It presents a company's unique selling qualities within immediately recognizable eye-catching calls to action and has a clear, easy-to-use menu.

Web Design in Flash

Impressive websites have been created to use far higher visual effects and interactivity levels thanks to recent web design improvements such as the advent of Flash animation and high definition video content. However, this 'high-end' web design comes at a cost; site designs that rely heavily on Flash content are notorious for being extremely slow to load. They frequently include a progress bar that moves across the web browser to indicate when the website will complete loading.

This is similar to the progress bars you may be familiar with if you use video editing or 3D rendering software or play games on a console where they are displayed as you wait for them to load. Even if a web page has high-resolution photos, animation, or video, most internet users do not want to wait 3 to 5 minutes for it to load. They want websites that are quick to load, informative, and have a lot of material. They would watch TV if they wanted to view an animation or video.

- AMAZON CAMPERFORCE

Amazon has a few Fulfillment Centers that hire RVers to help with their holiday season throughout the last quarter of the year. This is their busiest time of year, termed Peak Season, and all hands must be on deck to meet consumer demands.

Amazon Camperforce associates are RVers who have been chosen to work and have particular job positions and responsibilities, work hours, and benefits packages. We've worked at two different centers so far. In our first season, we worked at a Texas plant from October through December. We took jobs in Kentucky from November to December the following year.

Each season was unique because we were given new jobs and shifts; yet, the overall experience was pretty the same. If you're interested in working as a workamper, here's a rundown of what to expect:

Monotonous Work

During the season, camperforce associates are normally allocated to one of four roles: picking, packing, stowing, and receiving. Essentially, each function entails a set of tasks that must be done and then repeated throughout the day; before placing a product in the right storage compartment, stockers, for example, scan and verify it. Consumer orders are collected by pickers and sent to the packaging department.

Each work is critical to the company's success; but, doing the same steps for hours on end can rapidly become tedious. Fortunately, there were times when colleagues were asked to assist in a different department or handle other work in their field. Assignments are ultimately determined by customer demand and Amazon's overall needs.

Long Working Hours

Associates at Camperforce typically work 40 hours per week, 10 hours each day for four days. These hours may be extended on exceptional sale days, such as Cyber Monday or when the demand arises. In most cases, associates are allocated to either day or night shifts. One year, we were assigned to the night shift and the following day shift. We had never worked a graveyard shift in our previous employment, so the day shift was our favorite. We felt like zombies on the night shift since it was so taxing on our bodies and minds. The timetable was never something we get accustomed to.

Keep in mind that the commute to and from work is not included in these ten hours. Some RVers were just a short walk across the street from an Amazon warehouse, depending on their setup. Other RVers were camping in nearby parks, which were roughly a 30-minute drive away. Campground bookings are made ahead of time, and those that start working early (as early as August) get the first pick of the sites.

Aside from that, if you travel with pets as we do, it's a good idea to prepare for them while you're away from the rig. We had someone come by at least once to relieve our dog, and we checked in on our breaks through a CCTV monitor. Phones are not permitted in the warehouse, although employees are permitted to use them during breaks away from the manufacturing floor.

Quite a bit of standing

These long hours of repetitive work are accomplished on concrete floors while on your feet. Tennis shoes that are comfy are recommended. Initial work hours are decreased by half the first week to help prepare Camperforce workers for the long hours of standing.

Affordably compensated

Despite the drawbacks outlined above, why do tens of thousands of RVers continue applying and reapplying for jobs? The remuneration package is rather attractive. Amazon Camperforce hires are given a paid campsite, according to their website. All hours, including overtime and shift differential, are compensated. Each associate who completes their contract receives a bonus, as well as referral benefits. Many RVers save their wages and use them to fund their trips and lifestyle a few months after they leave. Winter in Florida appears to be a well-deserved break!

Products of All Kinds

The items are one component of the profession that helps to break up the monotony. Amazon receives and ships a wide range of items. We'd come across some pretty humorous and risqué products among the clothes, toys, and pantry items now and then. These were the most common discussion topics during breaks: What was the strangest/most unusual item you stocked/picked today?

Comradery

Given the large number of RVers hired as Amazon Camperforce workers, it's no surprise that we met most of our traveling companions while working. In between work hours, a lot of networking takes place. Many of our coworkers have pointed us in the direction of potential working opportunities or provided us with advice and knowledge about the lifestyle. We continue to communicate with one another on the road and share our experiences, which have taught us many lessons from which we can learn and improve.

- AMAZON FBA BUSINESS

"What Is Amazon FBA?" is a question that many people have. Let's look at a brief narrative of how Amazon FBA can help you take your online selling business to the next level to help me explain what Amazon FBA is.

Amazon FBA, or Fulfillment By Amazon to give it its full name, is a program set up by Amazon that allows you to utilize Amazon to warehouse and then ship your products (and always sell your items on the Amazon Site). Amazon FBA is simple, but it is also quite powerful, and it can help you take your business to the next level for very little money.

Consider the following scenario: you're busy sourcing products and have picked up some books, CDs, DVDs, Home and Beauty items, and a few new toys (Yes, items sold via Amazon FBA have to be either new or collectible). Now, you're probably thinking to yourself, "I wish I could buy more stock, but I don't have any more room at home." This is where Amazon FBA enters the picture. And it doesn't matter whether you start with a basic Amazon selling account or upgrade to a Pro-Merchant.

You return home and scan or list the things in your Amazon selling account as usual. You print out some bar codes, which you must place over the original bar code on the object after a few clicks (Yes, items will need to have a bar code or be listed on the Amazon site). After a few more clicks, you'll have a packing slip to place in the box or boxes. You then schedule a carrier pick-up, which varies depending on where you reside and how you pay - each country is different.

Then you finish the order and wait for it to be picked up; your item will be at the Amazon warehouse within days, being sold for you, and you can relax and bank the money. Amazon FBA handles payments, shipping, and customer communications; you must find more goods and deposit the funds.

Yes, Amazon charges a few extra fees. Still, they're little in comparison to the savings on shipping - remember, you're using Amazon's purchasing power, so no more Post Office lineups and no more bubble wrap and boxes to buy.

Many individuals are unaware that Amazon FBA allows you to ship to eBay and other buyers. Amazon does keep track of your purchases and delivers them to you. And for a fraction of the price, and in most cases, significantly less than you could do it yourself. The Amazon site in your country provides all of the pricing information. In your search engine, type "Amazon FBA."

Give it a go; you have nothing to lose and everything to gain by giving it a shot.

- RUN AN ETSY SHOP

Etsy is a global online craft market where people can advertise and sell everything from antiques to handcrafted items. Handmade items, vintage items older than 20 years, and crafts tools are all available for sale. Limiting the types of products that can be sold on Etsy not only makes it a fantastic place to sell these products, but it also makes it easier for shoppers looking for antique or handcrafted goods to locate what they want.

To succeed in this industry, you must understand how to market and sell your products. The first step, regardless of what you're selling, is to open an Etsy shop. Assume you have questions regarding what may and cannot be sold, as well as how to open an Etsy shop. In that case, you can look up instructions on creating a shop, updating billing information, modifying communication features, and more in the Seller Handbook on the site.

You can begin listing your things for sale after your shop is set up. Make sure you have beautiful, high-quality images of your products to pique the interest of potential customers. Close-ups and full photos of all products should be taken in a well-lit place so that clients can see what they're buying. Photographs in focus, taken in poor light, or don't show the entire product will almost certainly result in more sales than photos that are out of focus, taken in poor light, or don't show the entire product.

You should also devote some effort to developing precise and meaningful product descriptions. Customers that surf the website are looking for handcrafted or vintage things with a story to tell. Because Etsy has so many unique products, you'll need to use photographs and descriptions to convince potential buyers why they should buy yours instead of comparable products. To convert potential customers into committed buyers, you'll need a stunning photo and a comprehensive product description that details the product's specifications, how it was manufactured, and how it may be utilized.

You may also use Etsy's keyword features to increase the visibility of your products in searches. Choose keywords that are relevant to your product and make sense to your target market. Include terms that describe the product, its materials, and the people who will use it. If your type of goods meets their interests, words like "industrial" or "rustic" will appeal to them and drive them to your shop.

You can start promoting your products and shop on social media sites or through a blog after you've set up your shop, listed your products, and added targeted keywords. You may also use Etsy to promote your products and increase traffic to your website. Not only with your items but also with how you sell them to your target market. On Etsy, your creativity will help you make more sales and build a loyal consumer base.

- GRAPHIC DESIGNER

Artists who work as graphic designers utilize art and media to deliver messages for businesses and other groups. Print, the internet, other digital mediums, movies, and pictures are used by graphic designers to convey their message. They are aware of the finer points of art that contribute to the success of a design job.

Logos, brochures, websites, business cards, magazine and newspaper advertisements, and the overall look and feel of an organization's overarching design plan are all common responsibilities of graphic designers.

Graphic designers figure out what their client or organization is attempting to say and who their target audience is, then use graphic arts to successfully communicate that message.

Graphic designer positions necessitate an understanding of a company's product or service and its target demographic. This is why, to communicate with clients, these positions necessitate a particular level of professionalism.

Furthermore, graphic designers must know how to ask the correct questions to understand the company's mission and target audience.

They will also research the target audience, target market, and the company's or organization's offers before beginning design work.

Jobs in graphic design necessitate the use of both sides of the brain.

Graphic design jobs necessitate an unspoken level of artistic and creative talent. Most persons looking for graphic design employment, on the other hand, may neglect the need to be a professional business person. Graphic design tasks are no longer filled solely by artists. Designers are increasingly expected to be specialists in advertising, marketing, and communications.

They will also need to be able to communicate technical information to do their jobs. Graphic designers work on more than just art projects. They must also design layouts for annual reports, financial reports, market studies, and corporate development reports, among other documents. They must comprehend the data, tables, and charts they are attempting to graphically represent in publications. As a result, they know how to turn it into a graphic that effectively communicates with people.

Financial and other technical data, in particular, must frequently be simplified to appear as a clear visual. To accomplish this, a graphic designer will need to know how to communicate effectively with technical professionals such as those in the finance or research and development departments.

Software for Graphic Design

Graphic designer positions necessitate knowledge of the most up-to-date graphic design software tools. Depending on the type of publication they are working on, this would most likely contain the Adobe suite of applications such as Adobe Illustrator, Adobe Photoshop, Adobe InDesign, Adobe Flash, and Adobe Dreamweaver. Graphic designer positions frequently necessitate technical knowledge of one or more graphic design software products. Graphic design classes and degree programs frequently employ these graphic design software packages, which are frequently provided at a cheap cost at local community institutions.

Lay of the Land for Graphic Design Jobs

Graphic design employment can be found in a wide range of commercial settings. Some work in huge organizations' graphic design departments. Some graphic designers work for publishing houses, advertising firms, or print shops. Various graphic designers work for small to large design firms that contract out their work to other businesses and organizations.

About a quarter of graphic designers are self-employed and run their own business from home. Those who are employed frequently take on side freelance projects on their own time. Fully self-employed graphic designers are entrepreneurs who must manage all aspects of their firm. They must perform sales and marketing, billing and collections, and customer relationship management. Because of the pressure to generate cash for themselves, self-employed graphic designer positions can be more stressful. Many work greater hours than individuals who work for a larger design firm or a corporation.

When applying for graphic design jobs, applicants should have a portfolio of their work, either online or in print, to exhibit when they apply. These positions may even need you to audition by completing a tiny sample project as part of the application process. Graphic designers have the advantage of conducting freelance design work on the side in their spare time. Some design firms demand that their graphic designers handle all of their clients via them, while others do not.

Cross Over Careers

Some graphic designers move into marketing and advertising as a career path, while others leave the field entirely to manage a creative arts team. Some go on to work as management consultants in the design, marketing, and advertising fields. They can even establish their design and marketing consultancy agency if you're particularly talented and have good interpersonal abilities.

- VIDEO EDITOR

Video editing is a multidisciplinary job that necessitates a wide range of skills. This is not a game for the faint of heart. Video editors must be both creative and technically proficient. Given how quickly video-editing software changes in the film industry, all video editors must stay up with evolving technology first and foremost. Aspiring video editors may now learn Adobe Premiere software quickly and be on their way to new work, thanks to Adobe Premiere training sessions. Anyone who wants to work in video editing for a long time must quickly pick up new abilities, and no one can become comfortable with anyone sort of software. Professional video editors cut out the bits of a film that aren't needed, then piece it back together to create the continuity that any finished output requires. In certain circumstances, editors will sift through hours of material to piece together a film second by second. It's a demanding profession that necessitates personal qualities that no software can develop on its own.

Video workers will frequently work long hours, often alone and under tight deadlines. They must have exceptional attention to detail, strong stress management abilities, sharp problem-solving skills, and a keen sense of camera angles and special effects. Professional video editors must work around their schedules and have strong interpersonal skills, particularly in conflict resolution. They'll collaborate with sound editors, cinematographers, and directors, as well as the rest of the crew. Working on a smaller indie film will take a lot of patience and a lot of hard work. Although understanding the appropriate tools is essential, there is much more to video editing than that.

Amateur and hobbyist video editors will require different abilities or have the same potential for interpersonal compromises as professionals. People who make videos on YouTube and other comparable websites face distinct challenges and are held to different standards than professional video editors. YouTube videos are frequently produced on a shoestring budget, distributed for free, and consumed in rapid succession. Professional-grade films are held to high standards. Industry and even independent films are costly, and they expect to get what they paid for happy customers. Learning video editing software can be an exciting ticket to a very newfangled kind of fame in this age of Internet celebs. Even filming little movies needs meticulous attention to detail, camera angle knowledge, and a sense of time, among other things. Amateur video editors working on short films, on the other hand, are less likely to trawl through hours of footage. They'll be able to generate videos more quickly. Amateur video editors frequently operate alone, relying on their software abilities and imagination.

- FREELANCE (INSERT YOUR SKILL HERE)

For the past seven years, I've worked as a professional internet marketer in various online freelance marketplaces. I used to do all of my work on one marketplace when I first started my internet freelance job. I was able to maintain a comfortable standard of living throughout my work. I was able to secure much higher-paying freelancing employment when I started working on other sites. So, I'd want to give my perspective and the top 10 fantastic online freelancing marketplaces among the hundreds of freelancing marketplaces.

UpWork

One of the best online freelancing marketplaces is UpWork.com. This site combines two of the most prominent freelance marketplaces, oDesk, and Elance. A freelancer can find nearly any type of internetwork here. There are two types of occupations. One is hourly work, and the other is a job with a set price.

Freelancer

Another major online freelance marketplace is Freelancer.com. A freelancer might find work ranging from data input to high-level programming assignments here. Thousands of clients and freelancers can be found all over the world. Here, new freelancers can find the work they want.

Fiverr

Fiverr.com is, in my opinion, one of the most well-known online freelancing markets. In this case, a freelancer must publish a gig with detailed guidelines on what they can provide. If the client loves it, they can start with a five-dollar order. As a result, the client can easily obtain high-quality work at a minimal cost. As a result, our website is growing in popularity by the day.

PeoplePerHour

PeoplePerHour.com is a fantastic marketplace for online project freelancing. Assume you're an article writer, digital marketer, graphic designer, web developer, SEO specialist, or any other type of professional who enjoys working with their area of expertise. It's worth checking out PeoplePerHour. Clients will buy this and pay you according to your stated price if you post hourly.

99designs

This is a platform for freelance designers; 99designs.com allows you to compete in design contests and receive feedback from clients to choose the best designs and pay you well. It's an excellent method for exceptional designers to demonstrate their abilities while earning a substantial sum of money.

iWriter

The greatest online freelancing marketplace for content writers is iWritter.com. This is the quickest, simplest, and most dependable method of obtaining material for your website. For each high-quality piece, a freelancer might make over $15.

Job Opportunities for Freelance Writers

This is another popular freelancing site for freelance writers, editors, bloggers, publishers, and any combination of these. For freelancers with a knack for words, this is a fantastic alternative.

Toptal

For a custom software development project, Toptal.com is also one of the most prominent freelancing markets. A client might hire a highly competent and professional freelancer to provide custom software development services.

Project4hire

With hundreds of project categories to choose from, Project4hire.com makes it simple to find projects that match your skill set without having to sift through a vast number of job postings. It's ideal for authors, programmers, consultants, designers, and other professionals.

iFreelance

Some of the usual suspects in the freelancing sector can be found on the iFreelance.com website. Proofreading, artwork, data entry, graphic design, photography, accountancy, and other professional activities are available. However, freelancers will not be able to use this site for free. A membership charge will accompany it.

So, you may start your freelancing business or get your project done quickly by using one of these online freelance marketplaces. You'll find a diverse range of competent freelancers and clients from all around the world here. So, what do you have to lose? With these, you may begin your smart career.

- MOBILE RV MECHANIC

One of our favorite things about RVs is that most repairs can be done quickly and easily by the owner. However, there are situations when you may require assistance with a repair. When these larger problems emerge, many owners take their RV to a repair shop. Some folks, on the other hand, choose to use mobile RV repair.

Are you curious about mobile RV repair and whether it's a viable solution for you? This piece will walk you through the ins and outs of RV mobile repair so you can make an informed decision about if this is the option you want to pursue the next time your rig needs some TLC.

A mobile RV repair service, as the name implies, is a sort of repair service that comes to you. This could imply that a mobile RV technician comes to your campground or residence.

In certain circumstances, consumers seek this service since they cannot transfer their RV owing to damage. On the other hand, a mobile RV mechanic is frequently requested because it is the most convenient option.

Mobile RV repair services come in a variety of shapes and sizes.

Many individuals tend to think that a mobile RV mechanic is a "one-size-fits-all" solution. This is not the case, however. There are three different kinds of mobile RV repair services available.

#1: House Calls from an RV Dealer or a Repair Shop

On request, certain RV dealerships and repair shops will come to your home. This is usually only done in an emergency, and you'll probably have to pay a lot of money to have a tech from one of these places come to your house. As a result, if at all possible, we advise against taking this approach.

#2: Experts in RV Repair on the Go

Some repair technicians specialize in one form of repair over another. Due to their narrow customer base, these specialists frequently work out of their trucks, and if not, they are more likely to visit customers. However, because these repair professionals are experts, you should expect to pay a premium for their services.

#3: RV Service Technicians in General

Finally, there's mobile RV technology in general. This guy is a jack of all trades who has a little expertise mending just about anything that can go wrong on an RV. They rarely have a shop to work out of; thus, they only conduct mobile work. This is the individual you should call in most cases if you need mobile repair work done.

Obtaining Parts for RV Repair on the Go

You can't expect the general mobile tech (option #3) to have every RV part you could need on hand because they work from their truck. This means that the parts may need to be ordered online or picked up locally.

In some circumstances, the tech has connections and can negotiate a discount, so ordering through them is advantageous. However, ordering or picking up the required materials yourself often works just as well.

It may be better to speak with the repair person ahead of time to determine what you should get and have it ready to go when they come. This will save everyone time and, more importantly, money.

The obvious advantage of hiring a mobile RV tech is that you will not have to move your RV. There's no need to unhook and hitch up to have repairs done if you're already set up at your favorite campground.

Similarly, if your RV is parked in your yard, hiring a mobile technician eliminates the need to drive it into a shop. Finally, there's always the possibility that you won't be able to move the RV at all. This benefit is not only useful in these situations; it is also required.

Another great advantage of hiring a mobile RV repair service is that the work may be done in your yard, which means you may not even need to take time off work.

We also appreciate knowing that the technician will be solely focused on your rig while at your house or on your job site. This means you're less likely to make mistakes due to distraction, and you'll know exactly how much you're paying for hours spent just on your RV.

- GET PAID TO TAKE ONLINE SURVEYS

Many people become aware of paid online surveys and decide that they want to be paid for their time. So they apply to a few survey companies, answer a few questions, and then discover that the only way to "be paid" is to have their name entered into a "hat" for a drawing.

The winning prize for the drawing is supposed to be $1,000 or something similar. The number of people whose names are in the "hat" is unknown. The basic line is that they were "paid" in the form of promises and chances, not in the form of cash! This occurs much too often and affects far too many people.

"Life is a game where they throw you in without telling you the rules and then shoot you when you get off base!" Earnest Hemingway said it best. In the realm of paid online surveys, this is undoubtedly true. The purpose of this essay is to expose you to some of the "rules" quickly!

While practically every survey company claims to pay for surveys, only around 20% of the 700+ survey companies in the US and 3,000+ worldwide actually do so in cash or equivalent. You must identify the

20% of paid online surveys, sign up for them, and ignore the rest, the "time-wasters," to make money with paid internet surveys.

How is this even possible?

The large corporations that commission the polls pay the survey producers the full amount of the budgeted funds. Some survey participants receive a direct payment of a portion of the proceeds. Others offer participants little or no compensation in exchange for keeping the lion's share.

As a result, the second gang is continuously losing members and is forced to recruit new members. They reward everyone who can furnish them with recruits with money. Have you ever noticed the sponsored Google advertisements for "Free lists" of survey makers.

When survey makers offer payment to their survey participants, they rarely pay recruiting expenses. They are not obligated to!

As a result, it is not a good idea to use free listings. So, what's the best way to proceed?

Become a member of a reliable paid survey site advisory service. These membership sites maintain a list of reliable survey developers that they share with their members. For a small one-time membership fee, they will send you a copy of their current list (which you can recoup in the first 2-3 surveys). There are almost 200 of these websites available.

To identify a GOOD one, look for a strong money-back guarantee backed by a financial institution such as a bank, PayPal, or ClickBank. Then look for a warranty with a SMALL percentage of refunds. Customers were pleased with the value they received, as seen by the low refund rate. They're pleased because their list generated revenue.

High return rates imply many unhappy clients (who did not profit from the list they received).

You want to be among the satisfied clients (low refund rate), not the unsatisfied ones (high refund rate)!

To summary, look for companies who give STRONG money-back guarantees when paying for internet surveys. Look for one that you appreciate and has a low refund rate among this category (3-6 percent).

Avoid any refund rates that are either undetermined (another word for "high") or as high as 9-10 percent.

Any paid online survey site should be avoided unless it comes with a payment guarantee from a third party.

When you enter the world of paid online surveys, you'll have a far better chance of getting paid to take surveys and get paid!

- SELL GOODS AT FESTIVALS, FAIRS, AND RV SHOWS

Craft fairs, flea markets, and other venues are becoming increasingly popular places for people, particularly RV full-timers, to make money. People want a unique, handmade things that they won't find at Walmart or Target.

Vintage items, as well as the recycling and reusing of vintage items, have become quite fashionable. It's a perfect time for RVers who wish to sell their wares at craft fairs, flea markets, arts and wine festivals, and other similar events across their state or country.

It appears that converting outdated travel trailers and school buses into mobile stores is becoming popular. Some artists use the trailers as a mobile shop or workshop to make and display new works.

For a small sum of money, you can purchase an old, fixer-upper travel trailer. If you're willing to "come and grab it," you can sometimes find them for free. Moving a "free" trailer might be a pain because they normally need work before moving. It's possible that the taillights aren't working. The tires may be flat and rotten. The registration may be no longer valid. Even if you get a free trailer, it will still cost you money. If you want to make it into a mobile boutique, however, the investment should be cheap compared to the long-term profit.

Here are some suggestions for selling at craft shows:

1) Begin small. Don't go out and spend a lot of money if you're just getting started. Begin with a small booth to ensure that people are interested in what you have to offer. Invest in things like transforming an old trailer into a mobile boutique once you've demonstrated to yourself that you can earn a fair profit.

Begin with selling tiny, local performances. Keep track of the demographics of the people that buy your products. Is it a young or an older adult? Is it better to be blue-collar or white-collar? Is it a man or a woman? The objective is to get to know your clients so you can target them and choose shows where they're most likely to appear. To save money on overhead, consider sharing a booth with another company. When feasible, substitute imagination for cash in the beginning. Is it necessary to install hardwood floors in your trailer? Perhaps you could make something out of plywood, paint it, and then cover it in the hay. Make the most of the nice hay.

2) Take a stroll around the venue. Is this the appropriate shoe for the product you're selling? Is your work good enough for this show, or is it too good? Is what you're selling compatible with what everyone else is selling? Are you at a cat exhibition attempting to offer delicious dog treats? A panel of experts judges some shows. That means judges will examine your items and determine whether or not you will be able to sell them during the show. Interact with other sellers and inquire about their services. They'll give you recommendations and tell you which shows are suitable for you and which ones to avoid.

Book your shows as early in advance as possible to ensure that you have a good booth space selection. Because that's where people congregate, you'll want to be near the food court or restrooms. Keep a safe distance from live music. You can't talk to your potential consumers because it's too loud.

3) Analyze the Data You'll make money by selling your crafts at craft fairs. Calculate how much your normal overhead costs are. Costs might range from $10 at a school fundraiser to $800 at a huge event with a projected attendance of 75,000 people.

Other costs to consider include:

- Travel expenses

- The booth fixtures and decorations (table, chairs, lights, etc.)

- Your product inventories

- Permits and fees

Determine how much you'll need to sell to break even ahead of time.

4) There Is A Cost To Everything Make certain that each item has a price tag. Make an effort to have a reasonable price range. You want some affordable, easy-to-sell things, as well as more expensive items with a higher profit margin. Selling one item at $200 for a profit of $100 is easier than selling 100 goods at $2 for the same profit.

5) Credit Card Acceptance You'll lose sales if you don't accept credit cards, especially if you're selling things worth more than $20. Square Up, for example, allows almost anyone to accept credit cards. You'll receive a little device (a card reader) to connect to your smartphone. Enter the amount by swiping the card. It's that simple. The service fee is usually around 2.75 percent. If you swipe a $100 credit card, your bank account will get a deposit of $97.25.

- **DROPSHIPPING**

The most cost-effective approach for you to begin selling hard goods from an internet retail store is direct drop delivery.

Drop-Shipping takes place when a supplier follows the customer's orders for items not held by the supplier. The retailer transfers the customer's order to either the fabricator or a shipping wholesaler, which maintains an inventory of the product. The distributor or wholesaler now directly delivers the product(s) to the consumer (compliance) and pays the seller at the wholesale cost. The dealer who ordered originally billed the customer already at the retail price and reported the difference as gross profit.

Taking advantage Of Dropshipping

On-line drop delivery provides the obvious immediate advantage for retailers to establish and run a potentially strong, profitable company without the expense of purchasing and storing inventories of hard goods. However, the online retailer does not need to ship goods to clients and thus has no shipping department to manage.

Internet dropshipping logistics

You can run your e-commerce nearly anywhere, including the home office corner desks, without the need for storage and transport facilities. In addition to home office furnishings, your computer and printer are the only equipment available. All facets of the business are done through the computer-from the production of the site to suppliers and customer interaction. You can run your company from your home office or tropical beach while you are on holiday.

Online shipping start

When building your e-business plan money dropshipping, you need three main components for preparing an extra benefit.

1. Decide on what kind of goods you would like to market

2. Sourcing these products, which means locating reliable vendors for the items that you want to sell

3. Building not only a website but building a successful e-commerce business!

What Products To Sell?

Here you have the option of taking one of two roads. Selling hugely popular things such as electronics, health & beauty, shoes, jewelry, and so on is one option. The clear popularity of products in these locations indicates that the product you're selling competes in massive, high-demand sectors. That appears to be a great situation. However, this implies that there is a significant rivalry. Your market is vast once more, and if you are an expert marketer, you will do exceptionally well with your online business. If you are not at or near the top of your game, you may get lost among thousands of sites in your market.

Offering more specialized or "niche" products that don't have widespread demand or intense competition is one alternate sourcing approach. These smaller markets may be easier for you to control and rise through the ranks. Smaller markets would also be less price competitive, allowing for better profit margins.

Consider starting your decision-making process by looking inside and assessing your areas of interest or possibly hobbies related to products that others are looking for. Your knowledge of a topic may make your e-business even more entertaining.

- **AFFILIATE MARKETING**

Even if they haven't begun doing it, most individuals have heard of affiliate marketing. Referring consumers to various products and services on the internet is what affiliate marketing is all about. You get paid a commission for each sale you make using your affiliate link. The compensation amount is determined by the products themselves, who is selling them, and the percentage offered to the affiliate by the seller.

But what exactly does affiliate marketing entail? What do affiliate marketers do daily? How do they make money and learn what they should do?

A Successful Website As An Example

Online product and service marketing can be done in a variety of ways. Many affiliates start by creating a blog and then offer items and services through it. Moneysavingexpert.com is a popular website run by Martin Lewis. This is an affiliate website as well. Moneysavingexpert.com generates money by sending website users to various offers and creating material to help customers select which service to use: which credit card offers to chose, the best interest rate, and so on. If a sale is made due to this website, the link will be credited to it, and a commission will be paid. The website has established a name and grown in popularity over time through developing information, providing value, and assisting users in making informed decisions. Thousands of users visit the site every day to make shopping decisions, and Google ranks it higher in search engines.

How Do I Begin Working As An Affiliate?

Affiliate marketing is a massive industry. Thousands of people currently rely on the internet as their primary source of income. To get started as an affiliate, you'll need to master some fundamental ideas and develop numerous internet traffic methods for those offers. Many affiliate marketers begin with a basic blog. Many tourists keep a 'blog' about their journeys. If you don't know what to blog about since you don't have a love or interest, you can start by taking an online course. For further information, see my bio.

What Is The Average Time It Takes To Make A Living?

Some people use affiliate marketing to supplement their income. Some folks are looking to make a lot of money. The amount of time you can devote to your affiliate business and how committed you are to it will significantly impact your outcomes. The outcomes differ from person to person. Some affiliates have replaced their income in 6-12 months with large advertising spend and the proper business approach. Others may have to wait years until their current income is replaced. It can take anything from 3 months to several years to get it to the point where it can replace a current income, depending on your approach, advertising budget, and business plan.

Is it possible for anyone to do it?

One of the best aspects of affiliate marketing is that technology enables anyone to start their own internet business. Anyone who can send an email can use internet platforms and resources to start their own online business if they can study and apply what they have learned. The key requirement is a desire to study. Affiliate marketing, on the other hand, isn't for everyone. It does require a lot of effort, and you may not be rewarded financially for years.

What Are Affiliate Marketing's Pitfalls?

To make your affiliate company successful in the long run, you must devote some time to it. Some people believe affiliate marketing is a magic drug that will pay them in cash right away. You can't expect to receive more out of life than you put in, just as you can't expect to get more out of work. Affiliate marketing is based on results. This means that you will not be compensated until you can successfully sell products and services online. It can take years to do this if you don't know what you're doing. You can't expect to make a lot of money as a dabbler. Years of hard labor have resulted in large earnings. Expect to put in a significant amount of effort to attain this.

What Are The Most Beneficial Aspects Of Affiliate Marketing?

Affiliate marketing provides a great deal of independence and flexibility. You may work an affiliate business from anywhere in the world as long as you have a laptop and access to the internet. You can set your hours and schedule them around your current work. Many people get into affiliate marketing because of the flexibility it provides. They have the freedom to set their priorities in life, such as spending more time with family, setting their working hours, traveling, and working abroad. There will be no more commuting or working long hours for a supervisor you dislike.

Affiliate marketing also has a high degree of scalability. The number of people who can travel to a local business is always restricted. A global web business is possible. You can scale using tools and software to reach thousands of people using digital technology by combining digital products with a global reach. Much of the effort that goes into running an online business may be automated. You can focus your actions on reaching a wider audience through content production and paid advertising by incorporating automation into your company plan.

- **SELF PUBLISHING**

After finishing a book, an author must decide whether to publish it traditionally or independently. The majority of authors would give their book to friends and relatives or post it on a website that could be downloaded for free!

Isn't it better, though, if a book is published and a bigger number of people can read it and appreciate your work? Self-publishing is the simplest and most convenient method. Nowadays, an increasing number of authors are self-publishing their books. The following are some of the reasons why people opt to self-publish:

There will be no more rejection letters.

Why do you have to put yourself through the trouble of writing proposals to dozens of publishers only to get rejected? It will just make you feel as though your book is unworthy of publication. There will be no waiting, crafting a story summary for self-publishing, and no looking at the wall. You're going to publish your book right away!

One method to consider is self-publishing, then ensuring that the book sells well. If you still want a traditional publisher to publish your book, they will take you more seriously because of your track record.

You are in command.

Traditional publishers will make changes to your book to make it "better." You are the one who created your work. You are the one who wrote it. Why would you allow someone to edit your book just for their benefit? That's your tale, your concept, your imagination, and your hard work. You have complete control over your story if you self-publish your book. You are free to publish whatever you wish.

Most significantly, you are the sole owner of your book's copyright. So, without authorization from your publisher, you can sell, give away, or bundle your book in any way you wish!

You might be able to make extra money.

When compared to a traditional publisher, self-publishing your book may yield a higher profit. After paying for marketing and book printing, you should be able to keep all of the money. A traditional publisher will pay you 10% to 15% of the book's sale price. Remember that you have complete control over the pricing of your book, so you can decide how much profit you make on each one you sell.

Sell your book on the internet.

Self-publishing allows you to reach a broader audience. As with traditional publishers, you may sell your books on Amazon.com and Barnes & Noble. Readers may now transport thousands of books with them wherever they go, thanks to the invention of the Kindle and iPad. When you self-publish your book, you open up the possibility of being discovered in ways you never thought. Traditional publishers may be skeptical of your book, but after it's published online, you could be surprised at how many people enjoy it. Many prominent authors have also sold their books through their websites and profited handsomely from their sales.

Your book is a product of your efforts.

Your book is in your hands. Anything you want to do with it, go ahead and do it! Nobody will be able to stop you. Write whatever comes to mind. Make the cover exactly how you want it. It's all up to you. From beginning to end, you decide all of the decisions in your book. A good self-publishing firm will solely be there to help you with publishing services.

There are many horror stories about self-publishing out there; study them and learn from their mistakes. Simultaneously, there are many self-publishing success stories out there; be encouraged and follow in their footsteps.

CHAPTER 9: MYTHS ABOUT PASSIVE INCOME YOU CAN'T AFFORD TO BELIEVE

Every entrepreneur seeks passive income. Only a few people, however, understand how to distinguish between fact and fiction.

Passive income is one of the most intriguing concepts. After all, what could be more appealing than earning money without having to work? When you hear in the news that Amazon founder Jeff Bezos earns more than $230,000 each second, it's reasonable to question how you can make money when you are not working.

Even if you don't earn as much passive income as Bezos, having a second source of income could allow you to escape the 9-to-5 grind and pursue your business goals or travel the world.

However, generating passive income isn't as simple as some of the world's wealthiest people make it appear. It takes a lot of effort to figure out how to generate a consistent flow of cash. Even more significantly, it necessitates that you invest your own time and money in the appropriate areas.

Over the last decade, passive income strategies have earned a name for themselves in the investment industry. The name says it all: passive income. After you've done your due research, all you have to do now is sit back and wait for the checks to start rolling in. However, for whatever reason, some people are still skeptical about passive income strategies. Whether it's a case of ignorance or apprehension, there's just one thing you can do to overcome your fears: educate yourself. The more you understand passive income, the more likely you are to put one of its ideas into practice.

However, there are a few common misunderstandings that might lead to investor confusion. Unfortunately, it is due to these beliefs that many investors cannot realize true passive income and potentially endless wealth-building opportunities.

You can't afford to fall for these common falsehoods if you are serious about using passive money to improve your quality of life.

These common misunderstandings could be jeopardizing your investment attempts. So what are they? Perhaps more importantly, how can you navigate them to realize the potential your investing business has?

Passive income becomes the 'Holy Grail' for every investor at some time in their lives. Passive income strategies have an early impact on some people. Others wait until they're in their forties or fifties to start planning for the unexpected. Then many put off pursuing it until they are close to retirement, at which point panic sets in. Unfortunately, there are so many myths surrounding passive income that people might spend years going down the wrong rabbit holes. So, what are some common misconceptions surrounding passive income that need to be debunked?

1. You can "set and forget" your revenue streams.

This is, without a doubt, the most dangerous myth associated with passive income.

We all adore the concept of not having to do any more work after we've set up a blog or an online store. However, real-life is rarely so simple. Blog visitors to your blog want new content regularly. When students join an online course, they expect personalized assistance when they have a problem. The internet evolves at a rapid pace.

Your passive income can quickly dry up if you don't do your bit to stay on top of industry changes, client expectations, and other responsibilities that come with any "active" business. Even if you delegate responsibilities, you will need to check in with your team to ensure that tasks are completed to your satisfaction. To keep your idea relevant, you'll probably need to fine-tune it regularly.

Passive income still necessitates active presence.

2. You only need a single weekend to get started.

It's easy to believe that anyone can create a blog or another form of passive income in a single weekend. In reality, before you earn a single penny, you must do a lot of research and work to create a source of revenue that will last.

Even something as basic as starting a blog needs a great deal of research and planning.

, to get started, bloggers need to find the suitable niche, choose a web hosting provider, and purchase a domain name. After that, they must learn about browser caching, SEO, permalinks, and other topics — not to mention writing good content and uploading high-quality images!

Naturally, you won't be able to complete all of this in a single weekend.

Take the time to learn about the specific opportunities and challenges that your idea presents, and put forth the work to get it right. This isn't a race. Quality will always triumph over speed.

Serious entrepreneurs have two goals: passive income and multiple revenue streams.

3. One solid source of income is all you need.

Another dangerous misunderstanding about passive income is that you can make all of your money from a single source. It's the same as investing all of your stock market investment into a single company. I if that stock performs well, You'll be wealthy. However, if its values drop, you may find yourself practically broke.

It's a good idea to diversify your income streams, just like you should with stock market investments. This is particularly true if you want to use these income streams to replace your current job.

Bloggers with low web traffic, for example, use affiliate links and sell their items to supplement their revenue and give online courses and freelance writing services. You'll have a better chance of earning enough to cover your needs if you diversify your revenue streams.

4. Real estate is the safest form of passive income.

With home and property values rising rapidly across the country, many people believe that property management and home flipping are simple ways to generate passive income.

Successful property management is never truly "passive" in reality. Property repairs and renovations, dealing with bad tenants, and other unforeseen expenses are all too common, eroding the profit you hoped to make from such endeavors.

Property management and other real estate ventures rarely generate the expected return on investment (ROI). In fact, according to an infographic from Max Cash Home Offers, in a study done by the firm, one-third of all property managers indicated they "would not buy their space again."

Even "basic" personal finance tips like paying off credit card debt and maxing out IRA contributions become a better alternative for long-term financial stability due to management expenses. Selling a home rather than managing it is a safer (and easier) option in the long run.

5. You need a business idea to earn good money.

When you read about passive income, it's easy to get caught up in the concept that you need to start your own business or invest in real estate. However, this isn't always the case. Many people earn all of their passive income by simply depositing money into their savings and retirement accounts.

While such accounts may not appear to be as lucrative as a hot new business idea, they are a far safer option for those looking to fund their future ambitions. Most investors believe you should expect a 5% annual return on investment from your retirement plans.

That may not seem like much, but over time, if you continuously add to these accounts, the growth can be substantial. Saving a little more money each month might add up to a lot in the long run.

6. You'll naturally come up with great ideas.

"If you build it, they will come" may have worked in Field of Dreams, but it is rarely a recipe for success when starting a business that will generate passive income.

Even if you've done your market research and are confident that you're creating something people would enjoy, that doesn't mean they'll find your blog or product on their own.

For potential clients to find you, you'll need more than just a website. Supporting marketing channels such as social media, SEO, email lists, PPC campaigns, and even participation in industry groups and forums will be necessary.

Ensuring that clients find your "passive revenue" source requires action.

Don't hesitate to inquire about guest posting opportunities on other successful blogs to generate favorable awareness about your brand. The more you promote yourself, the easier it will be for the right people to find you.

7. You need money to start earning passive income.

Many individuals believe that obtaining passive income requires a lot of money, whether investing in the stock market or launching a small online business. This is not the case. You can invest as little as $1,000 in the stock market. For people looking to start their blog, web hosting is often available for less than $8 per month.

Having extra funds to get your blog or business idea off the ground can be advantageous. But the most important factor is your desire to commit the time necessary to analyze your market idea or investment opportunity thoroughly.

Doing your homework can help you make the most of your limited financial resources and earn a high return on your initial investment.

Create passive income the right way.

Chasing a dream of generating passive income isn't always easy, but it's not impossible.

Avoiding these common errors and misconceptions will go a long way toward helping you achieve your goals, whether you are trying to bring stability to your business or find a better approach to fund your retirement.

Success is closer than you think!

8. How little savings it takes to generate sufficient passive income

According to BankRate.com, individuals require at least $250,000 in retirement savings to earn $1,000 a month in passive income. Some people will find it difficult to save that much money. Few will live on such a low salary - especially when inflation and currency depreciation are included. This figure is based on a 5% withdrawal rate, equivalent to the rate of return used by mortgage lenders in crediting investment income when applying for a loan. While this may appear low to some, it may appear generous given how many people have lost on other investments. The fact is that passive income investments do not require as much capital as many people believe.

9. How much do you need

Many people may be grossly underestimating the amount of money required to begin investing in passive income properties. Some people may indeed need millions to retire. However, as Harvard Business School has discovered, investors who place a greater emphasis on income rather than nest egg size may achieve more with less. This is especially true for those who intelligently use leverage. For example, you may easily scale up to managing millions of dollars in assets and cash flows in real estate.

10. It takes a lot of work to generate passive income

Generating passive income requires some upfront effort. Some people believe that earning passive income is a very active pursuit. Some paths may be. However, they may not be truly passive income investments in that case. Even though many others are working behind the scenes to vet, package, and manage that investment, acquiring a passive income-producing investment can be relatively simple.

11. It means getting something for nothing

While some have tarnished the term "passive income" by promoting tacky "get-rich-quick" schemes, it does not mean getting something for nothing. There is a lot given to create passive income, whether it is hard-earned capital, sweat, time, or providing a service such as housing. Even if the ultimate goal is owning income property, each party gives something of tremendous value.

12. It's easy to make passive income online

Yes, it is possible. It can be easier to generate money online compared to many other things. On the other hand, making money online might lead to several detours that end up costing far more than expected. Some blogs and real estate organizations, for example, generate millions of dollars over the internet, but they have invested in content, design, and strategy.

13. I have to be invested in the stock market

Some people may find the stock market a good place to store a part of their retirement portfolio, and they may occasionally find reasonable dividends. It can, however, result in significant losses. Many people have amassed passive wealth and income without ever investing in stocks.

14. Crowdfunding

Crowdfunding can be a useful tool for investing and increasing income returns, but most people are still confused by it. Many of the most successful crowdfunding initiatives don't offer returns. Promoting your campaigns can help you build influence, but it takes a lot more time and money than most people realize. Most people would be better off sticking to direct private lending or direct investing.

15. Non-performing notes are an easy path to passive income

Non-performing mortgage notes might be excellent investment opportunities. They can provide good returns and, in some cases, can even be made to perform and create passive income for years. However, by their very nature and the reason they are so heavily discounted, they are already failing to deliver on the expected income.

16. Starting a business means passive income

It can if the structure is right. Owning a business, such as a real estate company, can generate passive income. This is, however, a far cry from the arduous work that goes into opening and running a mom-and-pop shop.

Passive income is vital, and it doesn't have to be as difficult to come by as these points make it seem.

CHAPTER 10: RVING WITH A PET

Pets and RVs just seem to go together for a lot of people. One of the main reasons for purchasing and traveling in an RV is to be able to bring your pets along. In fact, according to a Go RVing survey, 68 percent of RV owners travel with their pets. The majority, 92 percent, are dog lovers, with 14 percent bringing cats along on RV travels. There are many things to research, learn, and consider if you are a pet owner new to RVing or an RVer with a new pet to assist make traveling with your pet a good experience for both of you.

We traveled with two dogs a few years ago who have since passed away. Our West Highland White Terrier, lived to be 14 years old, while our Australian Terrier, died of cancer when he was 9 years old. They were diametrically opposite of each another. One is good, and the other is bad. One is shy, while the other is rambunctious. They only had one thing in common: they both enjoyed traveling in RVs. We learned a few things the hard way about traveling with pets when we first got them.

You know your pets better than anybody, but there are a few things to keep in mind when traveling pets in your RV. Our furry family members feel more at ease when their routine is followed as much as possible. With that in mind, here are some lessons we learnt about traveling with pets in our RV.

1. Take your pet's favorite bed with you

There's something comforting about the smells of home. When our dogs see their beds being hauled out of the house and into the RV, they know something exciting is about to happen. They are more comfortable in the RV because they have their beds. Fur Baby Tip: Stop periodically on your way to your destination so your pets can stretch and relieve themselves. We try to stop every few hours, at a minimum.

2. Crate Your Pet While your RV is on the Road

RVs do not have seat belts for our fur babies. Keep your pet safely tucked up in a pet carrier with a nice blanket or two while driving down the road, whether you're in a motorhome or a tow vehicle. An unsecured pet is vulnerable to a variety of dangers.

3. Food and Water

Take the food they're used to, as well as a couple of large water bottles filled with the water your dogs are used to drinking from home, so they may drink what they're used to. Water sources can differ from one location to the next, and just as a change in diet can disrupt their digestive system, so can water variations.

4. Vet Checks

Before you hit the road, make sure your pet is up to date on all vaccines and ask about any other health measures you should take. Did you know that your dog is susceptible to canine influenza? Dogs can get the virus at any time, but dogs that visit dog parks or come in contact with areas where many dogs gather are at a significantly higher risk of contracting it. When traveling, it's a good idea to get a flu vaccine. Bring your pet's records with you, including proof of rabies vaccination and a current health certificate. Make sure you have a recent photo of your pet if they get lost, and having them microchipped is a necessary precaution.

Fur Baby Tip: Ensure the chip number is registered with the National Pet Microchip Registration Database; your veterinarian can help you with this.

5. Ask About Pet Policies

When making campground reservations, always ask if the campground is pet-friendly and their pet policies. This information is often available online as well. Some campgrounds and/or travel destinations have Breed Specific Legislation (BSL) or insurance restrictions that prohibit dogs considered to be bully breeds. Ask about BSL laws at the campgrounds where you want to stay or do some research online.

6. Local Emergency Information

One of the first things we do when we arrive at the campground is check for the phone number of a local veterinarian and/or pet hospital in case of an emergency. This is simple to do using your phone or computer to look for a "veterinarian near me." Keep the information handy in case of an emergency.

Fur Baby Tip: If your local veterinarian offers this service, a pet portal will come in helpful. A pet portal allows you to log in to your local veterinarian's website and view all of your pet's records. Look into it before your trip. You can log in from your phone or computer, making it far easier to communicate with an emergency vet.

7. Protective Items

Bring paw booties! Ruffwear.com or Healerspetcare.com are excellent options. You'll want to keep their paws safe from the hot tarmac or sand, as well as any rough terrain you may encounter. We also bring a raincoat for our pets in the appropriate size. You wouldn't believe how unpleasant it is to have a wet pet in an RV. The raincoat keeps them dry and dry.

Fur Baby Tip: I keep a towel by the front door to wipe their paws as they enter.

8. Day Excursions

It can get extremely hot or cold in an RV. Always ensure that there is adequate ventilation, heat, and air. Make sure your pet has access to fresh water at all times. If your travel plans include day trips or extended travel away from the campsite, please bear this in mind. If we are only going to be gone for a short period, we play soothing music or put the TV on a channel that won't have loud sounds a. This helps to divert their attention away from the outside world. If you expect to be away from your RV and your pet for an extended period, consider a day at a local pet boarding facility or doggie daycare. Some campgrounds do offer kennels and boarding services for pets. Another issue is that you never know when the electricity may go out. You may buy pet monitoring devices that allow you to monitor the temperature and provide video and/or audio capabilities. If you choose this option, be sure you're close enough to the park or RV to return if something goes wrong.

Fur Baby Tip: If you're just going out for lunch or dinner, call and check; some restaurants with outdoor seating allow your dog to go with you.

9. Pet Etiquette and Tips

Make sure you're familiar with the campsite rules and any other location you are taking your pet. If you're going to use a tie-out anchor, make sure it's a good one (never leave your pet unattended). Allow lots of space for your pet to wander around, but be wary of traffic and obstructions that could cause them to become tangled. Make sure they are constantly leashed when you walk them or have them outside with you. Pet etiquette in the campground is a must. Be considerate of other campers when it comes to your pet. Always pick up behind your pet.

10. Creative Pet Containment

Some pet owners use creative pet containment systems to enable their pets to spend time outside with them. They must have access to shade and clean water. Make sure you are constantly in attendance when your pets are outside with you.

CHAPTER 11: RVING WITH KIDS

RVing with kids is a fantastic way to spend quality time with your family as well as new areas. However, as much fun as RVing with kids might be, it does come with its own set of challenges. The good news is that these tips for RVing with kids will help you overcome those obstacles and have a very memorable family RV trip.

Don't forget to include the kids when planning your next RV trip.

Before heading out on the road for your next family RV trip, you'll almost certainly need to do some planning. According to Camping World, if you're taking the kids, involving them in the planning process can teach them how notexpress themselves and listen to others and how to compromise.

"Have the kids do some research on places they'd want to go. Allow them to explain their thoughts and why they want to visit a particular location. You can give everyone a voice before deciding where to go next," Camping World explains.

Trailer Life has a similar take on the significance of planning as a family if you are RVing with kids. One of the best parts of planning an RV trip with kids, according to Trailer Life, is allowing your kids to help plan where you'll go, what you'll see, and where you'll stay.

Set expectations and get organized before you hit the road.

Getting organized is an important part of RVing with kids. RVs aren't the most spacious of places, especially if you're traveling with children. You likely have a lot of gear on hand.

"Create organized spaces for kids to store their toys, books, activities, or whatever else they chose to bring, and have them put their stuff away when they aren't using them," KOA advises.

Sit down with your children and talk about their expectations for the trip. Decide whether or not electronics will be allowed during your journey. Decide whether or not your children will be in charge of some camping chores. Giving your kids a primer on campsite etiquette is also a good idea, according to KOA.

You probably have many fun family activities planned for RVing with kids, from day hikes to smores by the campfire. But here is the thing: somedays, your kids might not want to leave the RV. Other days? You could encounter inclement weather that's not conducive to outdoor activities.

As a result, Trailer Life recommends setting up an outdoor play area and bringing games like Wiffle ball or ring toss with you. When it comes to rainy days? Make sure you have plenty of board games and playing cards.

"And if all else fails, throw on a movie and cuddle up." Trailer Life added, "Most RVs are completely equipped to watch a DVD or even stream from a phone."

With all of the activities you've planned for your RV trip with your kids, it's also necessary to relax and unwind. After all, organizing a trip and going is a lot of work.

Instead of always being on the go, Trailer Life recommends spending time with your family around a campfire, spending some time in a hammock, reading a new book. Or, better still, make use of that outdoor play area and play a good old game of ring toss.

Don't forget to have a good sense of humor when RVing with kids

Not every family RV trip will go according to plan. There will be mishaps and mistakes along the way. What matters most is how you deal with those mistakes.

Go RVing recommends packing a sense of humor when RVing with kids rather than stressing yourself out. "If something can go wrong, it will go wrong," they added. It's called Murphy's Law. Don't let it ruin your trip."

CHAPTER 12: RV MISTAKES YOU NEED TO AVOID

Everyone makes mistakes. Even the most experienced RVers sometimes forget to bring in the awning or properly latch the pantry. Unfortunately, some RV errors are more expensive and dangerous than others.

We've put together a list of RV mistakes to avoid in order to save you money on repairs and unpleasant experiences.

1. Going Too Far, Too Fast

Let's be honest. Not everyone has the luxury to go on a long RV journey. Most of us are simply trying to squeeze as much as we can into our two-week holiday period. On the other hand, a fast pace is one of the most stressful aspects of an RV journey. Driving from New York to the Grand Canyon and back during your children's spring break may have sounded like a nice plan at the time, but the fast pace of travel will eventually catch up with you. After all, if you drive for 6-hours every day, you won't have much time to enjoy yourself. Take it easy. Make a less ambitious plan. Make shorter journeys. Enjoy your RV.

2. Purchasing the Wrong RV

There's an RV for everyone out there. There's something for everyone from modest tow behind trailers to luxurious coaches with all the bells and whistles. You can find the right RV for your needs if you take your time and look at all of your options. However, if you hurry into it and buy the first RV you see, there's a good chance it won't be a good fit. Attend a few RV shows, poke around all the different types of RVs, and ask questions on online forums. Alternatively, you may rent an RV or two to get a sense of what you want and need. The ideal RV for you is out there; all you have to do is take the time to look for it.

3. Not Bringing in the Awning

Your RV awning is one of your favorites. It gives shade, privacy in cramped RV parks, and protection from the rain. However, the same awning is a notoriously temperamental addition. A few seconds of heavy wind and pounding rain is all it takes for a perfectly decent awning to devolve into a tangle of twisted metal and ripped fabric. The solution is simple. Bring your awning in at the first sign of inclement weather. Don't leave it out when you are not there, and do not trust the automatic wind sensors on the automated awning. When it comes to pricey RV awnings you are always better safe than sorry.

4. Forgetting to Disconnect

Oh no, they seem to have forgotten something! Have you ever witnessed an RV dragging an electricity cord or a sewer hose down the road? It happens more often than you might expect. There is a lot to keep in mind when packing up and leaving a campground. Disconnecting all utilities is one of the most critical things to do. Don't be this guy.

5. Being a Bad Campground Neighbor

You might be perceived as a bad campground neighbor if you carelessly dump your tanks leaving behind a mess for the next camper, don't pick up after your dog; you blare your music late into the night. Nobody likes to have a bad neighbor, and no one wants to camp next to one. Campgrounds are like small towns. If we're considerate of one another, then it's more fun for everyone.

6. Not Leveling the RV

No one wants to sleep on an angle. NO one wants to use the RV bathroom at a slant. Fortunately, this is a simple problem to address.

Just make sure your RV is level. The process differs based on the type of RV you have, but the core principle remains the same. Because you can't count on camping sites (even paved ones in luxury RV parks) to be level, let your RV do the job for you.

7. Packing Too Much

It's tempting to load as much as possible into your RV. After all, why not bring it if you have space? But here's the thing: Weight limits apply to RVs. When exceeded, limits can make driving – and stopping – your RV dangerous for you and other road users. If you stock your RV with a reasonable amount of supplies, you're unlikely to be overweight. However, if you start throwing everything in, including those five additional chairs, your enormous toolbox, and the massive cast iron dutch oven, you might be in danger. Make a list, cross things off that you don't need, double-check it, then cross off a few more items. After all, an RV journey is about the experiences you have rather than the possessions you carry.

8. Forgetting to Check and Recheck

Always check and double-check before driving your RV anywhere. Check the lights, the exterior compartment doors, and the trailer or tow vehicle connections as you walk around the rig. Ascertain that the television antenna or satellite dish is in position and that all windows and vents are closed. Check that all of the cupboards and doors are locked, that all of the items are neatly stowed, and that the refrigerator is closed. Before going along the road, make a list and go through it one by one. You can save yourself a lot of potential troubles and money by thoroughly verifying and rechecking each time.

9. Never Defrosting the Freezer

This may appear to be a minor thing. However, when you try to pack your RV freezer with fresh fruit and homemade lasagna to find it filled with an icy mass, you will be glad you took time to defrost. Residential freezers are not the same as RV freezers. Ice will accumulate at the back of the freezer over time, taking up valuable storage capacity and causing the freezer to malfunction. Defrosting the freezer is a straightforward procedure. Remove the food from the fridge and let the frost melt. You can speed up the melting process by using a hairdryer to save time.

10. Not Learning How to Drive the RV

RVs are not cars. They're large, tall, and heavy. You must learn how to drive your RV properly. Certain techniques, such as slowing down in severe winds, learning how to turn, and properly back up, will most likely take some time to master. Don't make a hasty decision—practice in a large empty parking lot. Consider taking an RV driving course or ask for tips and advice from your fellow RVers. Do not, under any circumstances, fail to learn how to drive your RV.

MISTAKES WE MADE DURING OUR FIRST YEAR

Things aren't always easy when it comes to RVing, especially if it's your first time. Prepare to make a few RV mistakes!

Before acquiring our RV and becoming full-timers, we had little experience with RVs. We thought we had done our homework, but we still made some rookie blunders in our first year of RVing. The good news is that you can prevent many of the issues we encountered by doing some research and planning ahead of time. I hope that you will be able to plan ahead of time and avoid the roadblocks we encountered. W below, whether you plan to buy an RV or merely rent one, you'll be a happy camper.

Rent an RV

Here are RV mistakes to avoid on your road trip.

Forgetting Important Things on Travel Days

Checklist for RV travel days

We learned the hard way to establish a checklist of steps to take to prepare for a move. A fifth wheel, sometimes known as a travel trailer, has more steps than a motorhome. However, no matter what rig you have, you should do a few things before taking off that can be detrimental to you and your rig if you forget to do them. These steps may appear to be "second nature" to you, but you'd be shocked how often you feel rushed or stressed on travel days.

It's easy to get a little flustered when you are cleaning up, packing up, planning your route, strapping down, and getting directions, all while keeping an eye on the clock to ensure you're done by checkout time. We've discovered that completing some activities the night before is beneficial. Enure you have enough gas in your tow car or rig the night before, so you don't have to worry about stopping right immediately. It's also a good idea to clean and stow or strap down items the night before. Give yourself plenty of time too.

The following items should be on your RV checklist:

Turn off the water heater and the water pump.

Raise the stabilizer legs (this is a step we've forgotten before!)

All of the windows and vents should be closed.

Check your brakes and turn signals.

Check the tire pressure

Make sure the tailgate is up (we forgot this once, too!)

Make sure you use it. If you are a couple, make sure each
person completes and checks off each item. After you've pulled away

from your place, have one person stroll around the area to make sure you didn't leave anything behind. There should also be a checklist for when you get to your new location. We've also had our fair share of such errors.

Not Knowing Exactly What You Need in an RV

We don't necessarily regret buying our first RV, but we wish we had been better informed and prepared. It's important to know what requirements you have for an RV. Consider your lifestyle and make sure the RV you buy fits that. We were limited in our ability to "boondock," or dry camp, because we didn't think about some features of our fifth wheel, such as holding tanks.

Need some help with a checklist?

From a general safety and preparedness standpoint, here's what you'll usually need in an RV.

RV registration

Insurance paperwork

Portable generator

RV owner's manual

Levelers

Tire pressure gauge

Jumper cables

Wheel blocks

Flashlight

Disposable gloves

Tool kitFirst aid kit

Camping chairs and table

Insect repellent

Bed linens for each bed

Sleeping bags

Sunblock

Clothes, based on weather and daily activities

Portable phone charger

Hiking gear, and don't forget the RV kitchen stuff:

Mixing bowls

Pots and pans

Cooking utensils

Bowls, plates, and cups.

Measuring cups and spoon

Plastic wrap, Aluminum foil, and food storage containers

Dish soap

Knives and a cutting board

Can/bottle opener

Cooking spray or oil

Paper towels

Fifth Wheel

Mistake #3: Trusting Google Maps and Not Validating Your Route

Many of us have gotten accustomed to getting directions on our phones. As a result, we often don't give much thought to the route it suggests. We'll usually just type in the address and leave without double-checking. You cannot do this with an RV. "As long as we are on highways, we'll be fine...truckers take those roads!" was the consensus. However, this is not always the case, and you should be extra careful on roads leading to and from highways.

Following Siri's instructions, we found ourselves in a stressful situation. We were directed to a highway that ran straight through a mountain as we left Sedona, Az. The roads were one of the most winding and tight we'd ever seen. Furthermore, numerous low-hanging trees were crashing on the roof of our fifth wheel. At that point, we realized we need to be more hands-on with our route planning.

Google Map RV navigation mistakes

We've seen many low clearance bridges and tunnels, as well as roadways with weight limits that appear out of nowhere. We recommend purchasing an RV-specific GPS to avoid getting yourself into a dangerous situation. Apps that provide maps with clearly defined regions with low clearance or weight restrictions are also available. We've made it a habit to double-check every road we'll be taking ahead of time. For this, we mainly use the All Stays app.

Mistake #4: Skipping the Practice Run Before Full-Timing

Our first time RVing was the same day we hit the road full-time. We were both apprehensive and had only intended to "learn as we go." Our first day was unforgettable... and not in a good way. Because of our lack of experience and the stress surrounding it, we made basic, careless mistakes. We regretted not doing a test run, even if it was just for a quick overnight camping trip close to home.

Fifth wheel towing practice

The only thing we did one evening was practice backing up in a parking lot!

We believe our first-day RV mistakes would not have occurred if we had gone for a practice run. We would have realized we needed a checklist at that point and could have avoided making foolish mistakes. We could have also practiced our roles and communication for parking. It's no different than playing a sport—there's way less pressure at practice than on game day! Overall, it would have boosted our self-confidence and calmed our anxiety. So, if you're a first-time RVer, do yourself a favor and get some practice time.

Taking a short road trip in a rented RV is one of the greatest ways to do this! It's a good idea to use rentals to learn the ropes and figure out what you like and dislike in an RV, especially if you plan on going long-term.

Take a road trip

Rearview mirror RV

We haven't looked back despite all of our "mistakes"! We wouldn't give up our RV life for anything!

Mistake #5: Going Too Far and Too Fast

RVing isn't just about the destination. It is also about having fun when you're on the road. Driving too far in one day will not only exhaust you, but it can also be dangerous. It's usually advisable to break your journey down in chunks and take breaks when needed. Similarly, don't try to push your RV to its limits. Take it slowly and cautiously. Trying to race to your destination at higher-than-intended speeds can result in unsafe conditions like trailer sway.

Slowing down allows you to appreciate your surroundings while also ensuring that you arrive in one piece.

Try It For Yourself

I sincerely hope that this chapter has provided you with useful advice for avoiding dumb mistakes during your upcoming RV travels. Now prepare that checklist, purchase an RV-specific GPS, and plan some practice time before your first trip!

CHAPTER 13: SECRET RULES FOR INVESTING AFTER RETIREMENT

How to invest money after retirement should be easy after years of investing for retirement. What should be one way is another, as with most "shoulds" in life—investing in anything but simple after retirement. Retirees must balance the need to identify safe investments to protect their income streams with the risk of running out of money in retirement. According to retirement experts, there are eight criteria for investing after retirement to help you find the right investments after retirement.

Be mindful of risk.

When it comes to investing in retirement, it might be difficult for retirees to reduce their risk appetite — after all, they've had decades of experience investing for growth. Patrick Murphy, CEO of John Hancock Retirement, says, "We see a lot of folks 50 and older chasing returns, taking on too much risk with their investments." "While a higher potential return is appealing, there isn't enough time to make up for any huge losses." He claims that a properly diversified portfolio is "critical to optimizing returns over a longer life expectancy while effectively managing risk to avoid severe short-term losses." He claims that retirees can receive income from the conservative portion of their portfolios while leaving the rest to grow.

Watch out for inflation risk.

While the risk of portfolio decreases should not be neglected while saving for retirement, retirees must also consider the risk of running out of money. "Even though inflation is low right now, retirees must keep up with inflation," says Jason Colin Patrick, principal of Fiduciary Advisors in Newport Beach, California. He specializes in corporate retirement plan advising services. "Most retirees will need to include equities in their portfolios throughout their saving years and into retirement." As a result, you may need to balance your desire for safe investments for seniors by having some growth-oriented items in your portfolio as well.

Think like Goldilocks.

According to Jeff Klauenberg, founder of Klauenberg Retirement Solutions in Laurel, Maryland, this dual-risk situation means you should invest in retirement like Goldilocks. The "just right" investment strategy entails not seeking a higher rate of return than is required for your retirement. "Why to invest for a 10% return if your retirement investment research suggests that a 5 percent average return will give your retirement lifestyle a high probability of success?" he asks. To help you keep risk in perspective, "separate what you need for retirement from any assets you want to build and pass on as a legacy." You can build the assets you don't need for retirement in this way without jeopardizing your future security."

Divide your retirement into five-year segments.

When it comes to investing beyond retirement, Klauenberg states that "no single investment can address the needs of a thirty-year retirement." Each five-year segment, such as 65 to 70 and 70 to 75, "has its specific lifestyle preferences and thus investment needs." He claims that money invested in the first 2 or 3 segments, during which time retirement income needs are affected by the bond and stock markets and the sequence of returns, should be invested more conservatively than money put in later retirement years. "Withdrawing income from a portfolio during a market downturn eliminates shares that will never be replaced," he argues. "Segments three through five can be invested for growth because they will have time to recover from negative or bad markets."

Consider real assets for diversification and inflation protection.

Real assets, such as REITs, commodities, and natural resource equities, infrastructure, according to Brian Cordes, senior vice president at Cohen & Steers, provide diversification, long-term return potential, and inflation protection. Real assets can help "defend against otherwise adverse market environments," according to Cordes because they have "generally fared well when both stocks and bonds have underperformed at the same time." He advises retirees to invest across multiple real asset classes for the best results: "While no single real asset class has excelled equally across total returns, inflation sensitivity, and diversification, investors can navigate those trade-offs effectively by combining them in a cohesive investment framework."

Look to preferred securities for tax advantages and fixed income diversification.

"Investors could consider matching high-yield bonds and/or municipal bonds with preferred securities to achieve a more diversified fixed income portfolio with lesser exposure to various risks," Cordes says. Preferred securities are a form of hybrid security that has both stock and bond characteristics. "Investors are paid more for subordination (having a lower claim on company assets in the case of liquidation), for the possibility that payments may be deferred or omitted (historically unusual in practice), and the general complexity of preferred securities," adds Cordes. He further points out that while most preferreds are taxed as qualifying dividend income, they are often taxed at a peak rate of 20% rather than 37%.

Have a drawdown strategy.

Switching from an accumulation to a preservation mindset while investing after retirement is a challenge. Making the most of your retirement investments and income sources becomes your investment goal. Murphy suggests that retirees use a drawdown plan to accomplish this. "By utilizing their resources in a tax-efficient manner and maximizing their Social Security claiming strategy," retirees can "increase the estimated lifetime value of their holdings." He claims that over half of retirees do not receive full Social Security payments because they claim before their full retirement date. "However, retirees can dramatically boost the lifetime value of their benefits by having a strategy in place, such as delaying when they claim," Murphy says.

Have an estate plan.

It's not just about you and your retirement income needs when investing after retirement. There are also your beneficiaries to consider. An estate plan is necessary to ensure that any inheritance you leave reaches your beneficiaries in the most tax-efficient manner feasible while still carrying out your objectives. "Estate taxes have been reduced recently, but they can and will most certainly be re," says Mark Charnet, founder and CEO of American Prosperity Group in Pompton Plains, New Jersey. He advises having these documents in order: a will that empowers your executor to carry out your wishes, a power of attorney allowing someone to act on your behalf in financial decisions, a health proxy allowing someone to act on your behalf in health decisions, a living will with advanced directives to physicians, and a living trust to avoid probate.

CONCLUSION

Even if you've never worked online before, these passive income possibilities are easy to implement and suitable for people of any age. All you need is a laptop and access to the internet.

It's a lot simpler than you believe. By being informed of the how-to's for the RV lifestyle, you'll gain confidence, inspiration, and feel unstoppable - because you are!

Avoid being intimidated by what others say about online work; their fear is based on ignorance. You must pay attention to your gut feeling. If your gut tells you that you are unhappy with your job and want to see more of the world, then you should follow your gut.

So, to avoid unwelcome surprises, a thorough discussion is required, which I tried to provide above.

I hope that all of this practical and realistic information gives you a broad picture of what it may be like to save money while living in a travel trailer and what you can expect from this lifestyle.

If you decide to go ahead with your plan and live on the road, remember to make it worthwhile! Remember to enjoy every second of it, click it, save it, and turn it into something amazing, but always stay safe and think practically!

The RV lifestyle is alluring, and it's achievable for anyone who knows what they're getting themselves into. Setting a budget for your purchase will help you locate a recreational vehicle that will provide you with years of enjoyment at an affordable price.

Your future is entirely in your hands, and all it takes is one giant leap to change the course of your life significantly. Your freedom to travel wherever you like is so close.

All it takes to achieve your dream is commitment and determination, as well as the necessary resources, all of which you must look no further for.

So, what are you waiting for? Follow your calling and ultimately live the life of your dreams!

www.ingramcontent.com/pod-product-compliance
Ingram Content Group UK Ltd.
Pitfield, Milton Keynes, MK11 3LW, UK
UKHW022151230426
12049UKWH00003BA/40